"Believers are given by God supernatural forged weapons of mass destruction against insidious evil works and to plunder the plunderer! In the power-packed and revelatory *Next-Level Believers*, Dr. Venner Alston thoroughly and biblically unpacks and exposes the stealth plans of the enemy. This book is truly a game changer for every Kingdom reformer, warrior and influencer who is armed and dangerous by the Holy Spirit, ready to bring the kingdoms of the world to become the Kingdom of our Lord and of His Christ in their generation and culture."

Dr. Hakeem Collins, founder, Champions International; author, *Unseen Warfare, The Power of Aligning Your Words to God's Will* and more

"*Next-Level Believers* is unequivocally the most revelatory and practical handbook written on the subject of warfare in a generation. She profoundly provides rules of engagement, apostolic strategies and prophetic revelation to arm all Kingdom believers with a fresh mantle for the next level of spiritual warfare."

Naim Collins, president, Naim Collins Worldwide

"At each breaking of a new era, Christians must learn how the Lord has chosen us as the necessary link to bring His will from heaven to earth. Once we understand the times, order and purposes that He is bringing from heaven, we will see a new authority begin to arise in each of us individually and corporately. This authority will cause us to be able to overthrow the enemies that have resisted us in past seasons. This is a time when *we must* continue to advance. Many do not recognize we are armed and dangerous—not with carnal weapons but with divine power to demolish strongholds. *Next-Level Believers* is a foundational guide that will establish your warrior call. We are in a time of 'going beyond.' This book will guide you into a new level of triumph!"

Dr. Chuck D. Pierce, president, Glory of Zion International Ministries; president, Global Spheres, Inc.

NEXT-LEVEL BELIEVERS

ADVANCED STRATEGIES FOR GODLY KINGDOM INFLUENCE

VENNER J. ALSTON

Chosen

a division of Baker Publishing Group
Minneapolis, Minnesota

Published by Chosen Books
11400 Hampshire Avenue South
Minneapolis, Minnesota 55438
www.chosenbooks.com

Chosen Books is a division of
Baker Publishing Group, Grand Rapids, Michigan

Printed in the United States of America

Library of Congress Cataloging-in-Publication Data
Names: Alston, Venner J., author.
Title: Next-level believers : advanced strategies for godly kingdom influence /
    Venner J. Alston.
Description: Minneapolis, Minnesota : Chosen Books, a division of Baker
    Publishing Group, [2022] | Includes bibliographical references.
Identifiers: LCCN 2021044477 | ISBN 9780800762377 (trade paperback) | ISBN
    9780800762636 (casebound) | ISBN 9781493435869 (ebook)
Subjects: LCSH: Influence (Psychology)—Religious aspects—Christianity.
Classification: LCC BV4597.53.I52 A47 2022 | DDC 155.9/2—dc23
LC record available at https://lccn.loc.gov/2021044477

Cover design by Rob Williams, InsideOut Creative Arts, Inc.

Baker Publishing Group publications use paper produced from sustainable forestry practices and post-consumer waste whenever possible.

22   23   24   25   26   27   28   7   6   5   4   3   2   1

This book is dedicated to the watchmen intercessors who
prayed and watched over me in the Spirit
throughout the writing of this book.
Every move of God is preceded by prayer.
It is my prayer and hope that those who read this book will
experience a profound move of God in their lives.
Thank you, watchmen intercessors.

Contents

Foreword

Indeed I will greatly bless you, and I will greatly multiply your descendants like the stars of the heavens and like the sand on the seashore; and your seed shall possess the gate of their enemies [as conquerors]. Through your seed all the nations of the earth shall be blessed, because you have heard and obeyed My voice.

Genesis 22:17–18 AMP

This powerful message was given to Abraham for his seed. We, the Ekklesia, are Abraham's spiritual seed. This promise to possess the gates of the enemy pertains to us. The gates of hell will not prevail against the Ekklesia—the Lord's sent ones and legislative Kingdom Body anointed to impact people and bring Kingdom influence and reformation to people, cultures, cities, regions, nations and spheres of influence.

There is a remnant that is rising up into the Kingdom inheritance we carry to possess the promised land of the harvest. We are citizens of the Kingdom of our heavenly Father. He has called us to be His ambassadors, ministers of reconciliation to see His Kingdom come and His will be done on earth as it is in heaven. The Hebrew word for "possess" is *yaras*. It means to be an heir, to take as an inheritance, dispossess, drive out, conquer, take possession (*Strong's Concordance* key #H3423). While some might feel uneasy with such strong language, allow me to give an overview of a few in the Word of God who functioned in obedience, contended against demonic structures and possessed spheres and gates of influence. Joseph possessed administration and finance in a completely pagan culture. Abraham possessed nations of the earth. Deborah possessed city gates. Daniel possessed the government mountain of Israel's enemy. Esther persevered and possessed life, freedom and victory for her people. David possessed a kingdom as a worshiper, warrior and king. Moses contended and delivered his people and possessed a nation. Joshua stayed in the tabernacle for forty years, was anointed to take action, contended against the enemies of Yahweh and possessed the promised land. Elijah contended against the prophets of Baal and possessed victory. Paul possessed cities, peoples, economies and regions. Peter possessed the lost, the Gentiles and cities.

This is quite a lineup of Kingdom-anointed glory carriers who functioned as reformers in their spheres of influence. Yes, they had their flaws. That was made clear in their life stories. However, their faithfulness and obedience to the Lord and His plans, their devotion in prayer and, in many of these instances, their ability to engage in spiritual warfare and press through resistance to rise as Kingdom influencers amid dark world influences were constant themes throughout the history of these Kingdom of God historymakers and reformers. It seems to me that each of these heroes of the faith had the mindset and understanding to pray, obey, contend, possess gates of influence and make great impact to extend the Kingdom of God. In my mind, this an awesome company to agree with and belong to!

Isaiah 62:10 tells us, "Go through, go through the gates. Prepare the way of the people; build up, build up the highway. Remove the stones. Lift up a standard over the peoples."

What does it mean to go through the gate? The Hebrew word for "gate" is *sa'ar* (*Strong's* #H8179)—the same word used in Genesis 22:17. I will share a few of its many meanings: a large or smaller court area, a specific location where people gather, a place where people meet for market and a place where legal business is done. It is clear to see that the term "gate" signifies an important meaning concerning a city, a region, the marketplace and legal business. "Gates" represent what we as His Ekklesia are to be as Kingdom influencers.

What does it mean to prepare the way, to build up the highway, to remove the stones and to lift up a standard over the people? To prepare, *panah*, means to turn away or reject an object and to take actions of any kind to make an event or state possible (*Strong's* #H6437). A highway emphasizes a journey of moving toward a destination. It also signifies conduct, meaning a way of life or what is done with great importance on strength. When we are maneuvering in His strength, as Venner so succinctly teaches, there is vigor, might, power, force and Kingdom authority. And through this strength we are to make ready, turn the way and cause circumstances to be prepared for His glory-anointed plans and Kingdom reformation.

I think we would agree that in all areas of society there are mindsets, ideologies, beliefs and practices that are idolatrous and ungodly in nature and hinder God's Kingdom from being extended. What is Isaiah indicating when he states to remove the stones? The Hebrew word for "stone" is *eben*. It means a piece of rock, an instrument used for an act of justice (*Strong's* #H68). It also signifies a stone idol, meaning a piece of rock, fashioned or not, that is worshiped as an idol. The good news is this word also represents a stone used as a building material.

Isaiah 62 goes on to tell us that we are to raise a standard, meaning to raise up, lift up. As standard-bearers we are to have hands lifted high, ready to take action when there is a signal or request for help. There is a calling not only to help but also to return to a safe position. Standard-bearers carry greatness, experience triumph and walk in honor. They function in the stance of warriors who are called to rise up in greater power against their foe, but who also build the new. When a standard is established, it saves and delivers from danger or dire circumstances. As the standard-bearers, His Ekklesia, we are to deliver, provide and give what is necessary to support and see divine increase. The light, life power, authority and voice of the standard-bearer overpower the sound of the flesh, the enemy, division and voices of the world. There is strength in the sound of what we pray, prophesy and release.

You and I are called to go through gates of influence in order to prepare the way. Through His strength, power and might, we create the thoroughfare toward Kingdom promise. We remove all idols, building a next-level model by functioning as His glory standard-bearers—His apostolic-prophetic Ekkleisa—to influence, to make impact, to empower true Kingdom disciples who deliver and save from dire circumstances, and to see His glory fill the earth.

Next-Level Believers is a powerful message filled with solid teaching of how we are to rise above the chaos of the world and the strongholds of division the enemy has established within culture. It empowers us to advance with strategies to bring forth godly Kingdom influence. This is a now message setting into alignment how we are to function in biblical form with Holy Spirit fire. Thank you, Venner, for this brilliant model that has been pinned with such anointing and Kingdom wisdom, revelation and clarity for this new era.

Rebecca Greenwood, co-founder, Christian Harvest
International, Strategic Prayer Apostolic Network,
and International Freedom Group

Acknowledgments

I would like to acknowledge Jennie Alexander, my dear mother, who went to heaven to be with the Lord as I embarked upon writing this book. Thank you, Mom, for being a powerful demonstration of a next-level believer who prayed and who declared the Word of God where you could, when you could. You were not an apostle, prophet, pastor, teacher or evangelist, yet you performed mighty deeds throughout your ministry. May we not only follow your example, but go beyond.

Introduction

God has a purpose and plan for humanity. To accomplish His plan, God established the Church, the Ekklesia, to represent Him as His voice in the earth. The fact that you are reading this book tells me you are passionate about fulfilling the destiny God has for you. The Church is not the building or the gathering place where meetings are held. The Church is comprised of believers like you who have received Christ as Savior and are living faith-filled lives of obedience to Him. That is the Ekklesia.

Armed with supernatural capacity, the Ekklesia is authorized and anointed to influence every sphere of society and fulfill the mandate of heaven to represent God on the earth. You are anointed to influence the sphere God has assigned you to. Matthew 16:18 (TPT) states, "And this rock [the truth of who I am] will be the bedrock foundation on which I will build my church—my legislative assembly, and the power of death will not be able to overpower it." The Church is anointed and positioned to overcome the dark powers attempting to hinder God's Kingdom mandate. This includes you. I want you to read the following declaration aloud. As you do, you are declaring your identity in the natural and spiritual realms.

I am a faith-filled member of the Church, the Ekklesia. As a believer, I represent the Kingdom of God through my life and ministry. I have been given influence and authority to overcome the powers of hell, and the gates of hell will not prevail against me.

In each generation and in every season, believers are to enforce the victories Christ won at Calvary. To accomplish this effectively, the Church must gain fresh revelation of spiritual warfare in every war season. War seasons occur throughout the span of your life. I describe such times as a season since there are also seasons of triumph, victory and rest from our enemies. Understanding how the warfare mantle changes from season to season can only be accessed through revelation. As you read the pages of this book, you will be gaining understanding and accessing revelation. Then once we have received revelation concerning the war mantle for a season, we must commit to wearing it. Lack of revelation results in using strategies and tactics that may have been effective in previous seasons, but are not effective in the new season. For every new season, our warfare strategies must change.

Why do we need a new war mantle? Nations are in crisis. Darkness is attempting to establish its image and agenda in every sphere of society. We only need to look at the redefinition of marriage to see the "imprint" of darkness. When I was growing up, family was defined as a marriage between a man and woman, which might or might not include children. Today, marriage has been redefined to include the same-sex agenda, an agenda that did not come from heaven.

Dear one, don't misunderstand my intent here. God loves everyone, and He sent Jesus to redeem all mankind from sin and destruction, according to John 3:16. This gift of salvation is freely offered to all and is received by faith. Anyone, regardless of lifestyle, addictions or other issues, can receive the free gift of salvation made available through the finished work of Christ. Acceptance of this free gift yields life changes that align with God's Word, the Bible.

Hell works to keep people in darkness, preventing them from seeing the truth of who God is and who He wants to be in them. If you have not received Jesus as your Lord and Savior, I encourage you to receive Him now. I believe that God, who loves you, led you to this book so that you would come to know Him. Don't be ashamed to receive Christ right now by praying this simple prayer:

God, I repent of my sins, and I receive Jesus, Your Son, into my life by faith. I believe that through the blood of Jesus, I am redeemed from sin. His blood cleanses me and makes me whole. I commit to yield my life to You each day and to live as one of the Ekklesia. Thank You for receiving me.

Just by praying this simple prayer in faith, you have now had your name recorded in the Lamb's Book of Life. I encourage you to get connected to a vibrant faith community where you can be strengthened and encouraged.

Darkness is escalating. Through our ministry as faith-filled believers who courageously commit to influencing our families, our workplace, our communities and everywhere else we go, we will overcome the darkness. The light of God's Kingdom will transcend and overcome the darkness through us, the Ekklesia.

Isaiah 5:14 (TPT) states, "The shadowy realm of death grows thirsty for souls and opens its mouth even wider to drink in the people!" Our influence is linked with authority. We must understand not only how to use the authority given to us to push back the darkness, but also how to use our authority and weapons to defeat the powers of hell and deliver those who are captured in hell's grip. Wherever darkness attempts to establish itself, the Church is authorized to unseat the darkness, replacing it with the light of the Kingdom of God. We are the light of the world. This is a picture of *influence*, which is defined as "the capacity or power of persons or things to be a compelling force on or produce effects on the actions, behaviors, opinions, etc., of others."[1] This influence happens as we walk fully in our identity, and we will discuss more about the power of walking in our Kingdom identity in chapter 2.

We can clearly see the nature of influence in Matthew 5:14–16, where the Church is described as the light of the world. Throughout the Bible, light is a major theme that appears repeatedly, both figuratively and spiritually. Looking at creation, we see that the first created thing was light (see Genesis 1:3–4). Beforehand, the earth was described as being formless and void, covered by darkness (see verse 2). God's response to the darkness was to create light. Revelation 22:5 states, "Night shall be no more. They need no lamp nor the light of the sun, for the Lord God will give them light." The source of the light is not within physical light itself. God is the Creator of light, and ultimately, He is the source of light. Because God is Light, by extension believers are also light. Without the Light, the world will remain in darkness. Let's look at ten biblical references to light and its relationship to God and humanity (although there are considerably more references in Scripture than these).

1. *God is Light.* God is Light, and in Him is no darkness (see Psalm 104:2; Daniel 2:22; 1 John 1:5). We who belong to God must take off the unfruitful works of darkness so that we can represent Him.

2. *Light transforms.* "For God, who commanded the light to shine out of darkness, has shone in our hearts to give the light of the knowledge of the glory of God in the face of Jesus Christ" (2 Corinthians 4:6). Transformation is linked with light. As we display the light of God, the

power of transformation is released. Those in darkness are transformed as they receive the light of His presence.

3. *Light is associated with safety.* During the exodus of Israel from Egypt, the Egyptians dwelt in darkness for three days, while Israel had light in their dwellings (see Exodus 10:22–23). Fear is an effective weapon the powers of darkness use. When people fear, they cannot see God. Despair and anxiety become a shroud of darkness that covers them. When we display the light of God, fear is displaced by peace, the shalom of God, which is linked with safety. In the midst of critical world events, wars, rumors of wars, pandemics, economic crises and the like, we must reveal the safety of God's presence.

4. *God covers Himself with light as a garment* (see Psalm 104:2). When the Church displays the light of God, we are revealing our God, who wears light as a garment. One of the characteristics of God is that He is omnipresent. This means that God can be everywhere at the same time. Wherever darkness exists, light has the capacity to overcome it. God's presence dispels darkness. As believers, we have the light of His presence within us. Regardless of where we are, we reveal the light of God.

5. *God is omnipotent.* Omnipotence means that God is all-powerful. God's presence is so powerful that darkness becomes as light. No matter what the circumstances, when someone receives God, the darkness that was once within is overcome by God's light (see Psalm 139:12).

6. *God reveals Himself in light.* When Solomon dedicated the Temple, the Shekinah glory of God filled it. The Shekinah was not a physical light, but a luminous cloud of light that filled the Temple (see 2 Chronicles

5:13–14). The Shekinah of God ascended on Mt. Sinai when Moses received the Law, and as Moses communed with God, the Shekinah (light) covered his face (see Exodus 24:15–18; 34:29).

7. *Righteous political leaders are symbolic of goodness and light.* Political leaders who are righteous and rule with fairness are as light and goodness to people. "He who rules over man justly, who rules in the fear of God, is like the light of the morning when the sun rises, a morning with no clouds, gleaming after the rain like grass from the land" (2 Samuel 23:3–4).

8. *Light is a symbol of blessings and goodness opposed to evil.* "For everyone who does evil hates the light and does not come to the light, lest his deeds should be exposed" (John 3:20). Prior to salvation, we wore the unfruitful works of darkness (see Romans 13:12). As part of the Ekklesia, however, you and I have taken off darkness and are clothed with the light of God.

9. *Light is a symbol of truth.* Revelation from God is light. Lack of knowledge or ignorance is a form of darkness. When revelation enters, light enters (see Psalm 43:3; 119:130).

10. *Favor is a symbol of light.* Favor brings joy and peace. The light of God's favor is always available to believers. "But the path of the just is as the shining light, that shines more and more unto the perfect day" (Proverbs 4:18). For example, Israel experienced joy and favor after defeating Haman (see Esther 8:16–17).

I am reminded of a scene from a science fiction movie, *Millennium*. The plot is based on futuristic time travelers who moved through time to correct tragic events in the past before they could occur and alter the future. The future earth had been devastated by pollution, resulting in people being unable to reproduce by having children. Throughout the movie, the futuristic travelers are working to correct past events that are affecting their future. When it becomes apparent that nothing more can be done, they make a decision to save as many people as possible. Everyone is instructed to "walk into the light." This is a picture of how you and I are called to influence cities, regions and nations affected by previous sin patterns that have resulted in generational iniquities and thrones of iniquity being established over these territories. We are called to display the light of the Kingdom, and ultimately, to influence unbelievers to "walk into the light of God" and become light to a world in darkness.

Wherever darkness exists, light has the capacity to overcome it. The transformation from dark to light is immediate; there is no negotiation. The only way darkness prevails over the light is when a malfunction occurs between the lamp holder and the lightbulb. You and I are lamp holders called to display the light of God through our lives. We are not the source of the light; the Holy Spirit is the source. Lack of submission to the will of God creates a malfunction that obscures the light from being revealed through us. But when we submit our lives to Him, His light radiates through us, changing the darkness in us and around us.

As influencers, we must take our place in the culture. We are not to be hidden. Our light does not belong in hidden places (see Matthew 5:14–16). Hidden light gives place to darkness. The Church has struggled to find her voice and her place in culture. In many instances, it appears that the Church has been assimilated into mainstream culture and has become secularized. When this happens, the influence of the Church diminishes as our identity becomes more and more reflective of culture and not of God's Kingdom. I see the secularization of the Church happening in these key areas.

1. *Increased factions versus unity.* Over the past years, the Church has become more politicized, coalescing around political parties and agendas to the extent of division and chaos arising among believers and even within families. The mere discussion of social justice or economic issues has created a divide within the Church. Two of the distinctions of the Church are love and unity. At an alarming rate, however, the Church has become divided. Division is an antithesis of unity and damages the Church's influence. A dichotomy exists between social/political opinions and unity within the Church. While everyone has an opinion, how do we become the Church, moving with the voice of God and speaking truth to power, without drifting into allegiances and loyalties to specific political personalities and parties to the detriment of Kingdom advancement? As next-level believers, we must position ourselves in our Kingdom identity. You must understand your Kingdom vantage point of being seated in heavenly places, speaking to and influencing culture from your heavenly seat. You can refer to this as supernatural seating that enables you to influence cities, regions and nations.

2. *Voicelessness.* Next-level believers release the voice and wisdom of God. Influence and voice are linked. When you lose sight of your identity, you lose your voice. Rather than boldly declaring the word of the Lord, you then cower in fear, seeking acceptance. Next-level believers are called to release a clear and distinct Kingdom message from generation to generation. Our message is not popular, but it is necessary. We are God's delivery system, His voice, called to carry His message. Without our message, the world will remain in darkness. There must be a way of communication, whether through books, podcasts, messages, and the like, that effectively

communicates the heart of God, influencing people toward His Kingdom agenda.

3. *Barrenness.* Next-level believers produce fruit that remains. You and I were created with the capacity for reproduction. God commanded Adam and Eve to be fruitful and multiply (see Genesis 1:28). Not only that, but every seed, herb and animal God created also possesses the capacity to reproduce (see Genesis 1:11, 22). When the Church's identity is more cultural than Kingdom in her expression, we lack influence and will remain barren. Too many organizations that identify as churches have become secularized. Their identity as the Ekklesia is often virtually nonexistent as they submit to cultural norms at the expense of their Kingdom identity. Tolerance and acceptance are preached and practiced at the expense of a balanced, powerful Kingdom message. These are barren institutions (see 2 Timothy 3:5; 2 Peter 2:17–18). They have a form of godliness but lack Kingdom power.

We are now living in a post-pandemic era. A new fluidity has affected our understanding of what it means to be normal. As new crises unfold, our understanding of normal continues to change. In spite of all the changes around us, our identity as the Ekklesia is not fluid. Our identity is established in Jesus Christ, our Redeemer, and does not change nor shift.

Culture has continued to shift farther from God, however, becoming more and more hedonistic. Current culture continues to advocate killing unborn children under the guise of choice, and also approves of terminating them later in the gestation period—making this abomination an even bigger atrocity. The abortion of unborn children is an attack against our future. Not only are we decreasing the population of humanity in such a heinous way, but also the blood of innocent children is crying out from the land, creating a curse.

Families are under attack, with marriage being redefined as something other than the legal union between a man and woman. To ensure the continuance of this diabolical assignment, sex education in public schools is being revised to facilitate the continued propagation of this distortion of God's intent. Under the guise of "gender confusion," kindergarten-aged children who are too young to understand the ramifications of this perversion are being influenced to embrace this deception. All the while, parents are finding themselves on the wrong side of the legal system as they parent their children from a biblical perspective concerning gender and other issues. I acknowledge the intermittent cases where a genetic injury occurs, resulting in issues that impact the clear gender designation of a child at birth. But let me state unequivocally that God, who is the Father of souls, determines our gender.

We can see that current culture continues to undermine parental authority. Another example of this is the American foster care system, which was designed to protect children from abuse, neglect and other family ills. Let me state here that there are cases in which removal from the home is equitable for children living in environments marked by abuse and neglect, which are toxic to their productive development. Removal in these cases is appropriate and necessary for the children's safety, of course. On the other hand, there appears to be a systematic but unwarranted removal of some children from homes where they reside with their parent(s) or another family member. Some parents are affected by a lack of employment, poverty issues, addictions or incarceration within the family. Others lack the capacity to navigate the complex foster care system and its requirements. Such parents can face the dim reality of losing their children permanently. The children are then placed in homes with strangers. In too many cases, after being placed in foster homes expected to provide better conditions, these children are subjected to even worse conditions. This weakens families.

Beyond this, in current culture there is an increasing intolerance toward the Ekklesia and God's Kingdom message that we have been given to carry. The Church is the authorized voice of God in the earth. Courageous believers committed to declaring a balanced Kingdom message of repentance are being labeled as intolerant, homophobic, xenophobic or any one of the convenient terms created for the sole purpose of silencing the voice of the Church. We are the Ekklesia, and in the face of this we must gain greater understanding of the authority God has given us. God has given us the supernatural capacity to accomplish His agenda.

This book will help you gain a greater understanding of the rights, responsibilities, gifts and anointings of the Ekklesia, and of how you must use your supernatural arsenal to advance the mandate of the Kingdom of God. Psalm 115:16 states, "The heavens belong to the LORD, but the earth He has given to the children of men." We are anointed and appointed to advance God's Kingdom mandate in our generation.

Global upheavals, the pandemic crisis, economic instability and social unrest have signaled the moment in time that the children of God must arise. All of creation is groaning, waiting for the manifestation of the sons of God (see Romans 8:22). This reference to sons is inclusive of women. As believers, we are the sons and daughters of God. The sound of creation groaning is not a passive sound; it is the call to war. We must arise now and allow the Holy Spirit to clothe us in a new war mantle for this season. From generation to generation the earth has groaned, calling for the manifestation of sons and daughters for that time. Can you hear it? You are being summoned to the battle for the soul of nations.

This is not just another book on spiritual warfare. The truths in these pages will give you a biblical foundation for and understanding of what you are called to do and how you are to execute your assignment. I have divided the chapters into three sections.

Part 1, "Wars and Warriors," provides a biblical foundation for understanding the battle between the Kingdom of God and the kingdom of Satan. Part 2, "Revealing the Reformers," outlines the role of apostles and prophets, who are anointed to equip believers and send them into what are called the seven mountains or cultures of influence. Part 3, "Armed and Dangerous," provides insight into the spiritual arsenal God has given every believer.

To help you apply the principles you will read about, I have included some prophetic decrees and confessions that you should read aloud each day. I have also included "Application" sections from time to time, which will help you apply the principles we are talking about to your daily life. At the end of each chapter, you will likewise find "Reflection" and "Prayer Activation" sections, which are spiritual exercises that will help you receive the revelatory truths contained in these pages. As you apply these truths, you will move beyond your last level of revelation and shift into the next level, advancing forward. We are called to advance and enforce the victories of Christ in the earth.

Finally, I want you to engage fully with these pages. Find your quiet places and quiet times to read and reflect. It is not by mistake that you have picked up this book. God has something He wants to reveal to you. Are you ready? Let's go!

PART 1

Wars and Warriors

The first section of this book is designed to give you a biblical understanding of the war against darkness and our role in it. Jesus is committed to building His Church, the Warrior Bride. If you don't understand that you are called to rule with Christ, you will remain passive and ineffective in this great war. The truths in these chapters will help you gain strength and revelation. Let's begin.

1

The War of Kingdoms

For our fight is not against flesh and blood, but against principalities, against powers, against the rulers of the darkness of
this world, and against spiritual forces of evil in the heavenly
places.

Ephesians 6:12

Understanding spiritual things is an area where many believers are deficient. Too many believers are under the
impression that the Church no longer needs to engage in spiritual warfare. If this is true, why does Paul, the apostle, address
the issue of spiritual weaponry and warfare in his letters to
the churches? The fact is, we are engaged in a constant battle
against the kingdom of darkness. This battle does not take
place in natural theaters of war—the conflict the Church faces
is not a conflict between flesh and blood. Our fight is not a conflict between nations, tribes, governments, gender or ethnicities,
although we can see the effects of the battle in these and other

areas. The battle you and I are engaged in is spiritual and takes place in the invisible realm.

The Bible commands us not to be ignorant of the schemes and tactics of the kingdom of darkness (see 2 Corinthians 2:11). Lack of knowledge of spiritual things opens the door of destruction into your life and ministry. God's Word states that His people are destroyed because of lack of knowledge (see Hosea 4:6). A key area of ignorance among believers is this area of spiritual warfare. Ignorance means to lack knowledge, and when we lack knowledge of spiritual things, we suffer defeat.

Satan is referred to as the "prince of darkness." Darkness is another reference to ignorance. Wherever you are ignorant, Satan can gain an advantage over you. This is why you must continually be filled with the Spirit of God so that you gain revelation and walk in victory.

Two Realms

"There is a natural body, and there is a spiritual body" (1 Corinthians 15:44). Two realms exist—the natural realm and the spiritual realm. Apart from understanding the two realms that exist, you cannot understand the invisible war between the kingdom of darkness and God's Kingdom. Both kingdoms are spiritual and are contending in the spiritual realm for control of the natural realm. Let's look more closely at these two realms.

The Natural Realm

We can perceive the natural world through our natural senses of sight, touch, taste, smell and hearing. All of creation exists in the natural realm and is tangible, meaning it can be experienced and it can be perceived. Everything that God created in Genesis is tangible and visible. When God created light, He said, "Let there be light," and light appeared (Genesis 1:3). Even with the creatures that fill the sea and earth, God spoke the words and living creatures appeared (see verses 20, 24).

You are a citizen of a natural kingdom located somewhere on the earth. You can perceive everyone in your environment through your natural senses. You can experience creation around you through your natural senses. The natural realm was designed to sustain natural life, and we live out the span of our lives in the natural realm.

Each of us lives in a natural kingdom of this world. Regardless of your physical location, you live in a town, city or village that is part of a state or nation. In the natural realm, rulership exists. Without government, chaos exists. There are governmental leaders—a president, a prime minister or perhaps a king or queen—who fill the role of sovereign leader over the people in your territory. Each nation is a "kingdom of this world." Since the fall of man in the Garden of Eden, rulership of the natural world and its kingdoms has been handed over to Satan, who exerts over them the power and influence of the kingdom of darkness.

During the temptation of Jesus in the wilderness, Satan offered the natural kingdoms of this world to Him: "Again, the devil took Him up on a very high mountain and showed Him all the kingdoms of the world and their grandeur, and said to Him, 'All these things I will give You if You will fall down and worship me'" (Matthew 4:8–9). Scripture also shows us that "the Evil One controls the whole world" (1 John 5:19 ERV).

The Spiritual Realm

The natural realm is the domain where people live and exist, and it is the place where much of our attention is focused. There is, however, a realm beyond the natural realm. It is called the spiritual realm. People are spiritual beings who live in a natural body. Created in the image and likeness of God (see Genesis 1:27), humans were created as cognizant, intellectual beings with the capacity to communicate with Him. Unlike other aspects of creation, when God created man, He fashioned him from the dust of the ground and breathed into him, and man became a living soul (see Genesis 2:7). The breath of God was the activation ingredient in the creation of man as a living being comprised of spirit, soul and body.

All of us have a natural body that lives in the natural world, but each of us is also a spiritual being with an eternal soul and spirit. Your soul and spirit are eternal. At the end of our natural life, we will live eternally. Those who have made Jesus Christ the Lord and Savior of their lives will live eternally with God in His Kingdom. Those who reject Jesus as Lord and Savior, choosing to live according to their own will and desires, will suffer eternal punishment reserved for the ungodly angels who aligned with Satan (see Psalm 9:17; Jude 8).

Three-Part Beings

Each of us is also a triune or three-part being: spirit, soul and body. "May the very God of peace sanctify you completely. And I pray to God that your whole spirit, soul, and body be preserved blameless unto the coming of our Lord Jesus Christ" (1 Thessalonians 5:23). Let's look at each of our three parts in a little more detail.

The Spirit

The first part of your being is your spirit, which is eternal. This "spirit of man" is the part of your threefold nature that contacts God. Another term for this part is your "inward man" or "the hidden man of the heart." This is the part of you that receives eternal life. Here are a few Scriptures that help illustrate this principle:

For the wages of sin is death; but the gift of God is eternal life through Jesus Christ our Lord (Romans 6:23).

Truly, truly I say to you, whoever believes in Me has eternal life (John 6:47).

He will give eternal life to all whom You have given Him. This is eternal life: that they may know You, the only true God, and Jesus Christ, whom You have sent (John 17:2–3).

I give them eternal life. They shall never perish, nor shall anyone snatch them from My hand (John 10:28).

We can see from Scripture that eternal life is the life and nature of God. God is the source of eternal life. "For as the Father has life in Himself, so He has given to the Son to have life in Himself" (John 5:26). The Word of God declares that the Son has the same kind of life that God the Father has. Jesus came that we might have life and have it abundantly (see John 10:10). The life of God that comes into our spirits is the nature and the life of God that re-creates our spirits and makes us new creatures in Christ Jesus. "Therefore, if any man is in Christ, he is a new creature. Old things have passed away. Look, all things have become new" (2 Corinthians 5:17).

As we just read in 1 Thessalonians 5:23, the Word of God tells us that we are to be kept blameless in spirit, soul and body. The spirit part of us, the "spirit of man," refers to our heart. In 1 Peter 3:3–4, Peter was referring to the human spirit when he talked about the "hidden nature of the heart":

Do not let your adorning be the outward adorning of braiding the hair, wearing gold, or putting on fine clothing. But let it be the hidden nature of the heart, that which is not corruptible, even the ornament of a gentle and quiet spirit, which is very precious in the sight of God.

Just as it is today, outward adornment was many people's focus in those days. Peter exhorted the Church not merely to be concerned with outward adorning, but with what was on the inside. Your inner man is the real person inside. Your outward man—the person of flesh and bones, your body—is not the real person. Your inward man—the eternal part of you—is the real person who will never die. "Even though our outward man is perishing, yet our inward man is being renewed day by day" (2 Corinthians 4:16).

The Soul

The soul is the seat of human intellect. It is the place where our mind, will and emotions reside. Your soul is the realm of your sensibilities and will, and it is the part of you that reasons and thinks. It deals with your mental realm. Your soul must continually be submitted to the Spirit of God.

> Stop imitating the ideals and opinions of the culture around you but be inwardly transformed by the Holy Spirit through a total reformation of how you think. This will empower you to discern God's will as you live a beautiful life, satisfying and perfect in his eyes.
>
> Romans 12:2 TPT

The apostle Paul's admonition to the believers was to allow the Holy Spirit to transform them inwardly through a total reformation of their thinking. Your mind is a key battleground of the enemy. If he captures your thoughts, it hinders your walk with Christ. Proverbs 23:7 states, "for as he [any person] thinks in his heart, so is he." The soul is the center of our mind, will, intellect, emotions, etc. Each day, you and I must commit to the transformation of our soul so that we are not conformed to the pattern of the culture. Our current culture has become hedonistic and self-serving. Even among those of us who profess faith in Christ, the transformation of our mind, leading to reformation of our lives, is too often shallow or nonexistent. Our lives must be reflective of the power of Christ working within us. The apostle Paul's message exhorted early believers that their experience with Christ must extend to the transformation of their entire lives. This fact has not changed. Your profession of faith in Christ must result in the total transformation of your life. This is a daily process that will continue throughout your life.

Your profession of faith in Christ is your starting point. You are to be transformed by the renewing of your mind. Transformation is a daily walk that occurs as our minds are renewed, or made new, by the Word of God. One of the greatest needs of the Church today is that God's people renew their minds with the Word of God. Just because a person is a Christian, and even is filled with the Holy Spirit, does not mean that he or she has a renewed mind. As Kenneth Hagin commented, "The mind becomes renewed with the Word of God."[1]

The Body

The third dimension of humanity is the natural man, or our human bodies. Unlike the spirit and soul, which are eternal, the natural body is not. The natural body is the "earth house" where our spirit and soul reside during our time on earth. The body, the natural aspect, has a span of time to exist in the earth, after which a person lives eternally in the spirit realm. Your body must be submitted daily to the Holy Spirit:

> I urge you therefore, brothers, by the mercies of God, that you present your bodies as a living sacrifice, holy, and acceptable to God, which is your reasonable service of worship (Romans 12:1).

The apostle Paul exhorted believers to submit their bodies to the Lord as their reasonable act of worship. This is something all believers are expected to do. Paul did not say to the Church,

35

"Pray and ask the Lord to make your body a living sacrifice." Rather, they were instructed to surrender themselves to God.

Prior to salvation, our previous habits and ways of living did not align with the Kingdom of God. These ungodly habits were reflective of the kingdom of darkness.

> But when you yield to the life of the Spirit, you will no longer be living under the law, but soaring above it!
>
> The behavior of the self-life is obvious: Sexual immorality, lustful thoughts, pornography, chasing after things instead of God, manipulating others, hatred of those who get in your way, senseless arguments, resentment when others are favored, temper tantrums, angry quarrels, only thinking of yourself, being in love with your own opinions, being envious of the blessings of others, murder, uncontrolled addictions, wild parties, and all other similar behavior.
>
> Galatians 5:18–21 TPT

As a believer, your reasonable act of worship is to surrender yourself daily to God. This means that you submit the activities of your body, the things that you do each day, to the Lord so that your life is reflective of a citizen of God's Kingdom.

Failing to submit yourself to the Lord diminishes your influence. How can unbelievers *see* Christ at work through you if Christ is not at work *in* you? As Kenneth Hagin put it,

> The choice is ours. We can let our body continue to dominate us if we want. That body, if we let it, will want to go on doing the things it has always done. Or we can choose to keep our body under control. Our inward man can dominate it and present it to God, a living sacrifice.[2]

Heavenly residence is not automatic, as people often suppose. The natural man is not eternal. All of us have been given a certain amount of time on earth. This is our life span. At the end of our lives, our eternal residence is determined by the choices we make during our earthly life. As I mentioned before, those who choose Jesus Christ as Lord and Savior of their lives are welcomed into heaven at the end of their days on earth. Those who do not are sentenced to eternal punishment in hell. Both heaven and hell represent spiritual kingdoms.

Application

Ask the Holy Spirit to show you unsubmitted areas of your life. As He shows you them, be faithful to repent and commit daily to submitting each area to the Lord. The Spirit of God helps us in the areas of our weakness. He will help you.

Understanding Spiritual Kingdoms

In addition to the natural kingdoms of this world, there are two spiritual kingdoms: the kingdom of Satan and the Kingdom of God. All of us are residents of one of these two kingdoms.

Satan is the ruler of the kingdom of darkness, where, according to Ephesians 6:12, a hierarchal structure of principalities, powers and rulers of darkness exists. The spiritual beings in the kingdom of darkness consist of demons and all the people who live in sin and rebellion to God's Word. Through the fallen systems and kingdoms of the natural world, the kingdom of darkness seeks to enslave humanity through the lust of flesh, the lust of the eyes and the pride of life. These spiritual forces of evil are at work in the world today.

Don't set the affections of your heart on this world or in loving the things of the world. The love of the Father and the love of the world are incompatible. For all that the world can offer us— the gratification of our flesh, the allurement of the things of the world, and the obsession with status and importance—none of these things come from the Father but from the world. This world and its desires are in the process of passing away, but those who love to do the will of God live forever.

1 John 2:15–17 TPT

God is the ruler of the Kingdom of heaven; there the Father, Son and Holy Spirit reside. Godly angels also dwell in heaven, along with the great cloud of witnesses, or those people who previously lived godly lives prior to their death.

We are to seek the righteousness of God's Kingdom every day and in every area of life. Our priority must be His will. Matthew 6:33 (TPT) states, "So above all, constantly seek God's kingdom and his righteousness, then all these less important things will be given to you abundantly."

The Scope of God's Kingdom

The Kingdom of God consists of God the Father, Jesus Christ and the Holy Spirit, as well as spiritual beings called angels and all the people who live in righteous obedience to God's Word. Those of us who live in that righteous obedience are called to influence those who are living in disobedience to God's Word. Luke 14:23 states, "Go out to the highways and hedges, and compel them to come in, so that my house may be filled."

The focus of kings and kingdoms is territory expansion—in other words, increasing the population of the citizenry and enlarging the territory. This is accomplished through invasion, conquering and domination. When this cycle is complete, the identity of conquered citizenry is reestablished in the new kingdom. We can see this pattern throughout the Old Testament. In Daniel 1, Nebuchadnezzar, king of Babylon, invaded and conquered Jerusalem. The wealth and citizens were confiscated and taken to Babylon. Upon their arrival, Daniel and his three friends were renamed, and they learned to speak Babylonian.

This process is called acculturation. We can also see this same process in God's Kingdom: ". . . giving thanks to the Father, who has enabled us to be partakers in the inheritance of the saints in light. He has delivered us from the power of darkness and has transferred us into the kingdom of His dear Son" (Colossians 1:12–13).

Although the natural kingdom where Daniel, Shadrach, Meshach and Abednego lived had changed, and their names and language had changed, their spiritual allegiance had not. In the midst of darkness, they did not waiver in their allegiance to the God of heaven. Their faith resulted in favor and promotion in Babylon as they used their position to exalt God, even in the midst of persecution. This is what next-level believers are called to do. You must use your influence to overturn the darkness. Don't allow yourself to become captured by and acculturated into the world's system. Rather, use your influence to compel men and women to come into God's Kingdom.

When we come into God's Kingdom, we begin to develop faith as we walk as citizens of that Kingdom. The Church is an expression of the Kingdom of God. His Kingdom is more than a denomination such as Baptist, Pentecostal, Lutheran, Methodist, Assemblies of God or any other denomination or network of churches. These organizations are manmade, established for the practical purposes of administration and organization. The Bible speaks of the true Church, which is not a denomination or a religious organization. The scope of the Kingdom of God extends beyond denominations. The true Church is composed of all those who have become residents of God's Kingdom.

In understanding the spiritual kingdom of darkness and the Kingdom of God, we must understand dominion. A kingdom has a ruler or king. The king is the central figure of the kingdom and is to be obeyed by the citizens. A kingdom has a domain or territory. The citizens are responsible to bring new citizens into the kingdom so that it is enlarged continually. Ancient kings fought to subdue other kingdoms so that their domain grew larger. This is a picture of territorial gains.

The Kingdom of God exists individually within every man, woman, boy or girl who has received Jesus by faith and has become its citizen. The Kingdom is expressed communally in the true Church, which is not limited to physical buildings or gathering places, but exists wherever God's people are. When the Church assembles, the Kingdom of God is expressed through righteousness, joy, peace, acts of kindness and demonstrations of God's power (see Romans 4:17; Acts 2:44–47).

The Nature of Our Battle

We do not fight our battle against flesh and blood. While we can spiritually perceive the manifestations of the kingdom of darkness, we cannot see the spiritual kingdom of Satan with our natural eyes. "Your hand-to-hand combat is not with human beings, but with the highest principalities and authorities operating in rebellion under the heavenly realms. For they are a powerful class of demon-gods and evil spirits that hold this dark world in bondage" (Ephesians 6:12 TPT).

Spiritual warfare exists because two spiritual kingdoms are at war. Each kingdom has citizens who carry out the agenda of their respective kingdom. It is important to understand that spiritual warfare is not a natural battle between flesh and blood. As Jesus said, "A spirit does not have flesh and bones as you see that I have" (Luke 24:39). Your spiritual battle therefore is not a battle against your family, friends, employer or any other people. This battle is not a battle of person against person; it is a battle against demonic spirits who do not have human bodies.

This battle is not a visible battle. It is an invisible struggle in the spirit world. It is a battle fought in the invisible spiritual realm, although it manifests itself in the natural realm.

Defining Spiritual Warfare

Spiritual warfare is the ongoing battle between the Kingdom of God and the kingdom of Satan. Satan is fighting for rulership of the earth and humankind. This battle is fought in the second heaven. If the "second heaven" is a new concept to you, here is how I describe it in my book *Next-Level Spiritual Warfare*: "The second heaven is the solar system (i.e., outer space). It is thought of as the stellar heaven, the place where the sun, moon and stars dwell. This is where powers of darkness reside, between heaven where God dwells and earth where mankind dwells."[3] This ongoing battle manifests in the earth in these ways:

1. As a *supernatural battle* between citizens of God's Kingdom and Satan's forces of evil. Paul declared who our opponents are whom we fight against as believers: "against principalities, against powers, against the rulers of the darkness of this world, and against spiritual forces of evil in the heavenly places" (Ephesians 6:12).

2. As a *cultural/social battle* between believers and the world systems that are under the influence of Satan. This dimension of the believers' battle manifests in cultural systems under the influence of antichrist spirits. *Antichrist* means to be against Christ. Anti-Semitism and the oppression of women are linked to the spirit of the antichrist. Social inequity, racism and prejudice are linked to the social war operating through the systems of the earth (see John 15:18–20).

3. As a *personal battle* between our human, fleshly nature and our born-again human spirit. Our human nature will not automatically submit to the Spirit of God. Through submission to God's Word, our flesh nature is brought under the rulership of the Holy Spirit (see Romans 7:23; Galatians 5:16–21).

As I previously stated, many believers do not believe that engagement in spiritual warfare is necessary. Yet the reality is that everyone is in this spiritual battle. There is no neutral ground where you are not at war. Your influence is a weapon of Kingdom invasion against the powers of darkness. Outside Christ, there is no "safe zone" where you are protected from the onslaught of the enemy's attacks. Unbelievers are captives of the kingdom of darkness. Another way to look at this is that unbelievers are prisoners of war.

Application

How do you see the kingdom of Satan operating in your life, family, ministry and nation? Make a list of things the Holy Spirit shows you and commit to praying daily over these areas until you see the Kingdom of God ruling in them.

The Issue of Ignorance

The enemy works to keep unbelievers in darkness (ignorance) so that they remain under the control of Satan. As 2 Corinthians 4:2–4 says,

> But we have renounced the secret things of shame, not walking in craftiness nor handling the word of God deceitfully, but by expressing the truth and commending ourselves to every man's conscience in the sight of God. But if our gospel is hidden, it is hidden to those who are lost. The god of this world has blinded the minds of those who do not believe, lest the light of the glorious gospel of Christ, who is the image of God, should shine on them.

Unbelievers can be found in every sphere of society. As an example, the political realm is one of the most powerful places for a person to be seated. From this position, those involved in politics can enact laws and legislation that can help advance or restrict the Church. As people and nations experience crisis, particularly global events, those who would seek to control its citizens in an ungodly way work under the cover of darkness and in partnership with darkness to war against the Church. Yet the Lord spoke this word to me: *The Church might be constrained, but My Church will never be contained.* I understood this to mean that no matter what restrictive measures are enacted to constrain the movement and voice of the Church, the end result will not be contained. Believers in the early Church experienced attempts against them to constrain their voice and growth, but the outcome was victory and growth as their influence increased.

Spiritual warfare is active participation in the invisible spiritual war. To engage effectively, you must have an understanding of both natural and spiritual kingdoms and their operations. How are both good and evil operating in every season? This is why the war mantle of the Church must change in every season. When you operate in an old war mantle, you will experience burnout and frustration. You must receive revelational, spiritual strategies for overcoming the enemy in your current season and place. In part 3 of this book, we will discuss our weapons of warfare and the rules of engagement in this war.

The Church cannot remain in ignorance concerning spiritual warfare. You must give yourself to consistent study of the Word of God and to prayer. When you increase your knowledge of Satan's strategies of attack, you become more effective in your warfare against darkness. Lack of knowledge in the areas of how Satan operates and the strategies he uses not only keeps you in ignorance, but it also causes you to operate ineffectively. You must understand what the Bible says about spiritual warfare, the scriptural basis of your victory over Satan and the forces of evil. You are called to intelligent combat. Intelligent combat requires revelation and understanding.

I am reminded of a principle of warfare used in the theater of war in the natural realm. Within military structure, each branch of the military has an "Intelligence Division." This division is tasked with gaining insight and information about the enemy's plans. Knowing where, when and how the enemy will attack is the focus of the Intelligence Division. Knowing how many troops and weapons will be sent is another key factor this division seeks to uncover. We can see this same principle at work in Numbers 13, when Moses sent twelve spies to explore the land of Canaan. If they were to possess the land God had given them, the Israelites would need intelligence on the capacity and tactics of their enemy. They could not operate in ignorance. This is a picture of effective engagement.

Next-level believers must also gain insight, revelation and understanding about the operations of the spiritual battle taking place between the Kingdom of God and the kingdom of Satan. A lack of understanding about the operations in this spiritual battle will result in defeats rather than victories. You are anointed to fight, war and win over the enemies of Christ! In our next chapter, we will discuss our supernatural identity. A key weapon of next-level believers is understanding who we are in Christ and the authority we have been given.

Reflection

Ask the Lord to show you areas where you might be operating in spiritual ignorance. Remember, ignorance means to lack understanding or to be in darkness. Satan dwells in the darkness and uses our ignorance against us. What don't you know that you need to know?

Prayer Activation

Lord Jesus, my eyes are open to see what You desire to show me. Give me understanding of the things I see. I refuse to operate in ignorance. I receive wisdom, revelation and understanding today and every day. I am a next-level believer, and by the power of the Holy Spirit I prevail over the darkness.

2

Our Supernatural Identity

Then He called His twelve disciples together and gave them
power and authority over all demons and to cure diseases. And
He sent them to preach the kingdom of God and to heal the sick.

Luke 9:1–2

Understanding your identity is key to walking in the authority God has given you. Who God created you to be and
what you are called to do are vital questions you must answer.
The authority you have is linked with your identity. God had
intention linked with your creation. That intention is called
purpose. God had something in mind when He created you, a
purpose for you. Your identity, purpose and destiny are linked
and are supernatural in nature.

Your life prophesies who you are and who you are becoming. Prophecy reveals God's intention. Your life is strategic and
timely. Psalm 8:4 asks of the Lord, "What is man that You are
mindful of him . . . ?" God preloaded your gifts and talents

into you before you were born. They are clues concerning your capacity.

Satan, however, seeks to mar your identity through trauma. Trauma damages your self-perception. When this happens, you cannot fully see who God intended you to be. Whether you understand your identity or not, Satan knows of your potential to damage his kingdom, and he will do everything he can to hinder you. He knows that every person born is a potential threat to his kingdom. Satan is not omniscient, meaning he does not know everything. His knowledge is limited. To prevent his own defeat by powerful believers, he therefore launches his attacks against humanity. But you can overcome such attacks because "He who is in you is greater than he who is in the world" (1 John 4:4). As a believer, you have the power of the Holy Spirit supernaturally infusing your gifts and talents. This supernatural infusion of His power enables you to fulfill the purpose for which you were created. It does not matter if your birth was planned or was a surprise to your parents. God created you with His intentions in mind. You were not born out of time; you were born for now.

Prophecy is a gift of the Holy Spirit given to the Church. Many believers operate in the gift of prophecy, as I do. When this gift is in operation in a believer's life, it is not unusual for that person to hear a word from the Spirit for other people, or for cities, regions or nations. I will talk more about prophecy in chapter 5, but right now, prophetically I sense by the Spirit that you may be reading this statement "you were not born out of time; you were born for now" and be struggling with what appears to be your untimely birth. If that is you, hear the Lord saying to you,

I am God, who orders time and lives. As I ordered time through the rising and setting of the sun, I ordered your birth. I invite you to lay down your angst over your birth. I speak healing into you from every hurtful word that was spoken over you.

Your life is not an intrusion. Your life was ordained by Me. I created you. I purposed you for now.

The identity God has given you longs for expression:

> He has made everything beautiful and appropriate in its time. He has also planted eternity [a sense of divine purpose] in the human heart [a mysterious longing which nothing under the sun can satisfy, except God]—yet man cannot find out (comprehend, grasp) what God has done (His overall plan) from the beginning to the end.
>
> Ecclesiastes 3:11 AMP

I have often spoken to individuals who have not connected with their identity and as a result feel unfulfilled in life. Church leaders can also find themselves struggling in a similar way if they are living with misplaced identity. You were created to defeat the kingdom of Satan. When you became born again, the power of the Holy Spirit activated the intent of God for your life in a new way. As a new believer, you were brimming with expectation. You were filled with the anticipation of new possibilities. A desire to be effective in the Kingdom of God was your daily expectation.

Do you remember that time? You wanted to preach the message of God's Kingdom to everyone. Your prayers were fervent and consistent—and then they were not. Your passion for living and walking as a supernatural believer had diminished. What happened? The enemy's attacks are subtle. A little at a time, you felt overwhelmed here, frustrated there, and suddenly, you found yourself in survival mode. But to thrive, not just survive, in the Kingdom takes a revelatory understanding of your identity in Christ. Knowing your identity and purpose is crucial because it will keep you passionate about walking in your God-given authority and defeating the powers of darkness.

Understanding Authority

Luke 9 gives us a picture of authority as Jesus gives His disciples two things: "Then He called His twelve disciples together and gave them power and authority" (verse 1). Jesus was the source of the authority the disciples were given. What was the source of Jesus' authority? We find the answer to this question in John 5:19, when He tells them, "Truly, truly I say to you, the Son can do nothing of Himself, but what He sees the Father do. For whatever He does, likewise the Son does." We find the answer again in John 12:49, when Jesus says, "For I have not spoken on My own authority, but the Father who sent Me gave Me a command, what I should say and what I should speak." Those who heard Jesus teach were astonished because He spoke with authority (see Luke 4:32).

Jesus received power and authority from His Father. Throughout the New Testament, He revealed the Father, who was the source of His authority. When you walk in the power and authority you have been given, like Jesus you reveal your heavenly Father. Just as Jesus was given power and authority, He then delegated power and authority to the disciples, and also to the Church and to you.

Let's look at the word *power. Strong's Concordance* key #1411 translates *power* as *dunamis*, meaning miracles, particularly "miraculous power." *Dunamis* is also translated to mean "ability, abundance . . . (worker of) miracle(-s), strength, power, violence, mighty (wonderful) work."[1] The second word we want to look at, *authority*, is translated in *Strong's Concordance* key #1849 as *exousia*. The meaning implies a sense of ability and is conveyed as "privilege" or "force, capacity, competency, freedom." Further, *exousia* is translated as "superhuman," "delegated influence," "jurisdiction, liberty, power, right, strength."

The word *apostolos* conveys the meaning of being sent as a fully authorized delegate of the sender.[2] (We will more fully discuss the anointing of those who are "sent ones" in chapter 4.) The disciples were sent with power *and* authority. They were given supernatural strength and might. Jesus had given them supernatural authority (*exousia*) to become superhuman individuals. As Barbara Yoder says in her book *Mantled with Authority*, "Power is strength, might, and ability. Authority is different. It is the delegated, and therefore legal, right to be and do something. . . . Authority is power in conjunction with who the person is, not what the person does."[3] You are a part of the Ekklesia. As such, you have been given the necessary power and authority to accomplish God's will.

Looking closer, you can see that authority, influence and jurisdiction were delegated to the disciples. *Jurisdiction* refers to territory. Jesus sent them into regions where there were cities, villages and towns. Their assignment in Luke 9 was different than the assignment of John the Baptist, who was sent to the wilderness. In his book *Apostolic Expansion: The Kingdom War for Territorial Gains*, apostolic leader Alain Caron writes of the disciples,

> They had not been chosen to attend a rabbinical school sitting and listening to the principles of a new doctrine, to receive a certificate. Instead, they were enlisted for a mission that began with a training camp followed by a hands-on field training course.[4]

The disciples were sent with power and authority. Both of these terms are connected to identity. These men were authorized and empowered. They represented delegated authority. In other words, when the disciples showed up, demons were served an eviction notice and sicknesses were healed as these believers preached the message of the Kingdom of God. Delegated authority means the one sent is fully authorized by the sender. Any words spoken or actions taken on the part of the sent one are representations of the sender.

What were the disciples given power and authority to do in the cities where they were sent? According to *Clarke's Commentary*,

> The word power means the power to work miracles; and that authority by which the whole demonic system was to be subjected to them. . . . The demons were to be cast out and the diseases to be healed.[5]

The Twelve were an extension of Jesus' ministry; He had given them delegated authority. As sent ones, they were deployed into villages and towns for a specific purpose, which again, we find in Luke 9:1–2 when He "gave them power and authority over all demons and to cure diseases. And He sent them to preach the kingdom of God and to heal the sick." The disciples were given power and authority over all demons *and* to cure diseases. You can see that Jesus made a distinction between demons and sickness. The disciples were also sent to preach the Kingdom of God. Jesus fully expected that they would accomplish their mission. After all, He had given them the power and authority to do so. As believers, you and I have been given the same power and authority.

Next-level believers have revelation and an understanding of their identity in Christ. This revelation gives them understanding that they are not called to be pew sitters, but to be city shakers. You have been deployed for the purposes of the Kingdom of God. Apart from understanding your identity, you cannot complete your mission. Precious one, you and I are described in the Scriptures over and over. The Word of God refers to us as *sons of God*: "Yet to all who received Him, He gave the power to become sons of God, to those who believed in His name" (John 1:12). In some translations, the word *children* is used instead. Let's look at a few additional Scriptures that support this truth of our relationship with God as our Father:

You are all sons of God by faith in Christ Jesus.

Galatians 3:26

Because you are sons, God has sent forth into our hearts the Spirit of His Son, crying, "Abba, Father!" Therefore you are no longer a servant, but a son, and if a son, then an heir of God through Christ.

Galatians 4:6–7

Do all things without murmuring and disputing, that you may be blameless and harmless, sons of God, without fault, in the midst of a crooked and perverse generation, in which you shine as lights in the world. Hold forth the word of life that I may rejoice on the day of Christ that I have not run in vain or labored in vain.

Philippians 2:14–16

Beloved, now are we children of God, and it has not yet been revealed what we shall be. But we know that when He appears, we shall be like Him, for we shall see Him as He is.

1 John 3:2

The Spirit Himself bears witness with our spirits that we are the children of God, and if children, then heirs: heirs of God and joint-heirs with Christ, if indeed we suffer with Him, that we may also be glorified with Him.

Romans 8:16–17

These Scriptures and others like them settle the question of who you are. You are a son or daughter of God. As a son or daughter of God, you are a joint heir with Christ. In essence, Jesus is your elder brother. This means that you share in His inheritance.

It is important for us to consider some important aspects of our identity as the children of God. Here are a few of those aspects for your consideration.

1. *Women are sons, too.* Although Scripture refers to sons, it is inclusive of women. We are the children of the Most High God. Both male and female believers bear His name and His image.

2. *Our identity is supernatural.* Humans were created in the image and likeness of God. We are cognizant, intellectual beings. Our identity, purpose and destiny are supernatural.

3. *Our identity is prophetic.* Next-level believers understand that the truth of their identity is prophetic. This means we were born with the intent of God within us—what He has declared. It speaks not only to who we are, but also to who we are becoming. When we yield our lives to God, the purpose He intended before we were born manifests.

4. *Purpose and identity are linked.* Your identity speaks of the unique purpose God created you for. The primary reason you were created is to advance the Kingdom of God as you are deployed against the kingdom of Satan.

5. *You are more than a showpiece.* While it is true that God created you and me for His pleasure and delight, this does not mean that we are simply a precious item that sits on the shelf of life as a showpiece. I like to use the analogy of toy soldiers. We are not decorative toy soldiers. You and I are armed and dangerous. This is an inherent characteristic of next-level believers. We embrace our identity as skilled warriors anointed to defeat the kingdom of Satan.

You were created to represent Christ in the earth, defeating the darkness, healing the sick and preaching the message of the Kingdom of God. It is time to stop believing that you cannot preach the Gospel, heal the sick or influence anyone for God's Kingdom.

In spite of the fact that our Father wants us to be secure in His love and in who He has created us to be, many Christians remain uncertain or conflicted about their unique, personal identity. Next-level believers not only know who they are in Christ; they also believe they can do what the Word of God says they have been anointed to do. Identity and purpose are manifested as you walk in your destiny. Every aspect of who you are and what you are called to do was predetermined before you were born.

Just as He chose us in Him before the foundation of the world, to be holy and blameless before Him in love; He predestined us to adoption as sons to Himself through Jesus Christ according to the good pleasure of His will, to the praise of the glory of His grace which He graciously bestowed on us in the Beloved.

Ephesians 1:4–6

Next-level believers are secure in their identity, understanding that they gain greater confidence through embracing by faith who God's Word declares they are. God has given you a unique identity and purpose, which is the foundation for fulfilling your Kingdom mandate. If you are insecure or unsure of your identity, reflect on whether or not any of the following behaviors are problematic in your life.

1. *Lack of personal confidence or self-worth.* If you are struggling with self-rejection or feelings of inferiority, this could be an indicator that you are not secure in your Kingdom identity.
2. *Negative self-talk.* Fear, doubt, rejection and envy are connected to negative self-talk. You believe what you tell yourself. If you are constantly degrading yourself, or if you are constantly subjected to being degraded by others, over time your self-perception will be affected. When this happens, your self-image will not align with

God's Word. This leads to feelings of unfulfillment and can hinder you from fulfilling your Kingdom mandate.

3. *Fear of man.* Letting other people's expectations of you set your direction can put you in a position of compromising the Word of God. It is also a form of ungodly control. "The fear of man brings a snare, but whoever puts his trust in the LORD will be safe" (Proverbs 29:25). Prophetic counsel from mature prophets or leaders can help you secure your identity in Christ so that you are being led by the Spirit of God.

Authority and Voice

Authority is expressed primarily through the words we speak, as well as through our thoughts and actions. During Jesus' earthly time, power and authority were dominant characteristics of His ministry. Here are a few Scriptures to support this truth:

For He taught them as one having authority, and not as the scribes (Matthew 7:29).

They were astonished at His teaching, for His word was with authority (Luke 4:32).

They were all amazed, so that they questioned among themselves, "What is this? What new teaching is this? With authority He commands even the unclean spirits, and they obey Him" (Mark 1:27).

One of the primary ways Jesus demonstrated His authority was through His teaching. He did not speak with fear or apprehension. Next-level believers understand the power of their voice, too, and the supernatural creative capacity within their voice. Dear one, if you are bound by a spirit of fear that is keeping you silent, it is time for you to be set free! This is my prayer over you:

I command every spirit of fear, insecurity, anxiety and fear of man that has held you captive to "release you and let you go!" I command your voice to be unlocked. Now, receive your freedom, in Jesus' name.

Everything in the earth is "voice activated," meaning that when words are spoken, a response is forthcoming. The same holds true even when we are speaking to ourselves. There is a response. *Strong's Concordance* key #5456 provides a meaning for *voice* using the word *phone (fo-nay)*. This word carries the meaning of "tone or language." While there are numerous forms of communication—print media, television, social media, and the like—the primary form of communication is verbal, through our mouths. We can use our voice either to bless or to curse. Words have creative power. This creative capacity is inherently prophetic. In other words, when we speak, there is a prophetic nature to what we say. Something shifts and changes in response. Things that were not previously manifested come into manifestation as we continue to speak.

I believe the Lord has ordered your steps to read this book. I believe your faith is being enlarged in amazing ways. Prophetically, I hear the Spirit of God saying to you,

You are in the season and time of a mind shift. I am breathing upon your mind, through every cell of your brain, and I am shifting old mindsets. The way you perceived yourself in your last season is shifting NOW, and you will see yourself from My perspective. The old is gone, and the new has come!

Dear one, receive the power of this prophetic word and declaration, in Jesus' name.

Our Creative Power

Let's continue our examination of the creative power of our words and how they are linked with authority. "In the beginning God created the heavens and the earth. The earth was formless and void, darkness was over the surface of the deep, and the Spirit of God was moving over the surface of the water. God said, 'Let there be light,' and there was light" (Genesis 1:1–3). The Bible gives us a picture of how God created everything in the created order by using words. When God spoke the words "Let there be light," the only recourse was for light to appear. Each time God spoke the words "Let there be . . ." what He called *to be* had to appear.

Humans were created for fellowship with God and each other. Created in the "image and likeness" of God, Adam and Eve possessed creative ability. God created them as speaking spirits. "Out of the ground the Lord God formed every beast of the field and every bird of the sky, and brought them to the man to see what he would call them. Whatever the man called every living creature, that was its name" (Genesis 2:19). God brought each animal to Adam to see what he would call them. Because Adam was created in the image and likeness of God, he was able to assign a name to each animal, bird or beast of the field. Whatever Adam said they were, that is what they became.

That is creative power! Adam spoke forth the animals' names, which coincided with their nature, and that is what the animals, birds or beasts of the field became. Adam prophesied what each thing would become. This is what prophecy looks like. Through revelation, we understand God's intent and we declare it. Names reveal identity and nature. God created each creature, and Adam prophetically knew what each creature was and named it accordingly. You and I, as descendants of Adam and Eve, possess the same ability. We, too, are speaking spirits.

Understanding the Creative Voice

Although Adam and Eve transgressed in the Garden of Eden, the creative nature of God remained in them. Our words carry creative ability. Not only are our words creative; when we are born again, we receive the Holy Spirit, who is prophetic in nature. As we declare the Word of God by faith, the Spirit of God infuses our words with supernatural capacity. As we seek God in prayer and worship, the Holy Spirit within us reveals the heart, mind and intent of God for our life, family and ministry. God's Word in us overturns every voice trying to overcome us. This is how God's narration, or His voice, operates in our lives. As God speaks, we gain understanding of His intentions for us, and of our unique identity and purpose.

When we speak God's Word, His authority fills our words and His supernatural force (power) is released through us. This is a picture of influence in action. God's voice is powerful, and no force on earth or above the earth can defeat the voice of the Lord! Consider these passages that help us understand this truth:

> The voice of the LORD is over the waters; the God of glory thunders; the LORD is over many waters (Psalm 29:3).

> The voice of the LORD sounds with strength; the voice of the LORD—with majesty (Psalm 29:4).

The voice of the Lord is full of majesty. What does this tell us about God? *Strong's Concordance* key #1926, *hadar*, defines *majesty* as "splendor," "comeliness, excellency," "glory" and "honour." Additionally, *majesty* in key #1921 means "to favor or honour, be high or proud." *Vine's Expository Dictionary of New Testament Words* provides additional definitions from the words *megaleiotes* and *megalosune*. Together, these words form the translated word *megas*, meaning "great or greatness."[6] *Megas* is used to describe God the Father, signifying His greatness. He is the Majesty on High. There is no other voice that is higher than God's voice. With God's voice comes His unlimited power, which can shatter every demonic narrative trying to influence you.

As I stated earlier, everything in the earth is voice activated. Everything in the created order has ears, and this means creation is listening. How will the earth recognize the sons of God? By our words. Not just any words, but our creatively powerful, prophetic words that manifest God's Kingdom. Jesus demonstrated this fact when He commanded the fig tree to wither:

> Now in the morning as He returned to the city, He became hungry. When He saw a fig tree by the road, He went to it but found nothing on it except leaves. He said to it, "Let no fruit ever grow on you again." Immediately the fig tree withered away.
>
> When the disciples saw it, they were amazed, saying, "How did the fig tree wither away instantly?"
>
> Matthew 21:18–20

Jesus demonstrated His power over creation when He spoke to the fig tree and commanded it to die. When Jesus spoke the assignment of death over the fig tree, the tree was still alive. But the instant Jesus spoke, saying, "Let no fruit grow on you ever again," the tree started dying. The tree had heard Jesus speaking to it and had responded. The disciples were astonished when the fig tree died; however, Jesus fully expected that it would. When you speak, whatever your voice has been directed toward must respond. For example, I have several natural plants in my home. One of my sisters, Jan, has taken the position of personal caretaker to each plant. She has named the plants and can often be heard speaking tenderly to each one, commenting on its growth and beauty. Needless to say, each plant is thriving. What we speak to, in accordance with God's Word, will thrive. The Bible is filled with God's promises to us. He has given us promises concerning our health, our families, our finances, our nations and so much more. In Matthew 17:20 Jesus stated, "If you have faith as a grain of mustard seed, you will say to this mountain, 'Move from here to there,' and it will move. And nothing will be impossible for you." Jesus linked faith with our words. Find the promise in God's Word about something and come into agreement with it. Let faith arise each time you declare the Scripture you have found. God's promises are true and will manifest His will. Keep speaking until you see a response manifest in the natural realm.

The problem is that too many believers don't understand who they are in Christ. They are ignorant concerning their identity. The prevailing thought among many Christians is that the power and authority Jesus and the disciples demonstrated was only for that time. Believing that you don't have the same voice of authority and power that they demonstrated leads to defeat. If you are struggling with feelings of defeat, you won't exert the Kingdom influence you have been given. Your life as a believer will be lackluster and lackadaisical.

Dear one, God has purposed you for greatness. You are anointed to influence your environment. Wherever you have been purposed to occupy, you have power and authority to influence those in that environment. Identity is powerful, so the enemy works to keep you in ignorance concerning who you are in Christ and the power and authority you have been given.

Application

Take time to consider areas of your life and ministry that are barren. Make a list of unfulfilled promises that you are waiting to see manifested. Find promises in Scripture and commit to speaking the Word of God over these areas until you see manifestation.

Speak Up

As I have established, lack of understanding concerning our identity is a manifestation of ignorance. Another way to see ignorance is as darkness—if an area of our understanding lacks knowledge, this is darkness. Not understanding who you are and the power and authority you have been given creates spiritual stagnation. Stagnation occurs when there is no movement. We were created to walk in Kingdom power and authority. Our voices should manifest the influence we have been given. Too often, we don't have the expectation of a response when we speak. We will examine this further in chapter 8, when we discuss faith. I will say here, however, that we have been given the Holy Spirit, and therefore the same supernatural manifestations that we see in the New Testament are possible for us to see today.

Manifesting this level of power and authority must become common among believers. I believe power and authority are characteristics of next-level believers. Our identity, authority and power are all linked with our voice, as is our influence. They all play a part in us fulfilling God's purposes. God has placed you strategically in your family and community as a divine change agent, with supernatural power to speak up and influence everything around you. Everything in the earth realm is voice activated. You have been given authority and power to overcome Satan's kingdom because Jesus, the Greater One, the Greater King, is with you! When you speak, the supernatural power of God wraps around your words, penetrating the atmosphere. Every seed brings forth fruit in due season. The centurion in Luke 7 described authority well when he told Jesus,

But say the word, and my servant will be healed. For I myself am a man placed under authority, having soldiers under me. I say to one, "Go," and he goes, and to another, "Come," and he comes, and to my servant, "Do this," and he does it.

Luke 7:7–8

Keep speaking the word of the Lord. Walk in the authority that you have been given.

In Mark 4, Jesus and His disciples needed to take a boat trip to their next destination, which was on the other side of the lake. Jesus said to them, "Let's cross over to the other side" (see verse 35 TPT). In this statement, we can see His intention: *We're going to the other side of the lake.* His statement was also emphatic: *We're going . . .* Once they were underway, Jesus sat down in the boat and went to sleep. As the boat crossed the lake, a storm arose. It is important to understand how the enemy responds to your words. Satan will work to create a false impression that what you have spoken will not manifest. The boisterous winds created fear and panic in the disciples. They had just watched Jesus teaching the multitudes and healing the sick. Demons had been screaming and crying out, "You are the Son of God" (Mark 3:11). A man with a withered hand had been healed (see verses 1–5). In spite of this, when the wind began to blow, rather than remembering what Jesus had said about going to the other side, the disciples surrendered to the fear of death. They forgot what Jesus had declared and allowed their fear to short-circuit their faith.

Regardless of the condition of your assigned territory, you have the authority and power to operate there. There is an "other side" in your community. There is a redemptive purpose of God waiting to be revealed. Your family, region and nation are waiting for you to operate in the realm of power and influence that God has assigned to you. Lives will be changed as you embrace your supernatural identity. You have been established in your territory as an earthly kingdom influencer for the Kingdom of God.

> From one man, Adam, he made every man and woman and every race of humanity, and he spread us over all the earth. He sets the boundaries of people and nations, determining their appointed times in history. He has done this so that every person would long for God, feel their way to him, and find him—for he is the God who is easy to discover! It is through him that we live and function and have our identity; just as your own poets have said, "Our lineage comes from him."
>
> Acts 17:26–28 TPT

The light of God shining through you in demonstrations of power and authority is your tool to turn your family, region and nation from darkness to light.

Remember this truth: When God said "let there be light," there was no alternative other than for light to appear. The disciples were so afraid in the boat that they accused Jesus of not caring about them. How many times have you and I done that? On our way to the fulfillment of God's promises, a contrary wind occurs, an unexpected circumstance, and we immediately form a wrong perception. It is at this point that you find yourself saying, *God doesn't care about me*, or telling yourself, *I won't get through this crisis; this is the end of my story.*

Dear one, these are lies of the enemy. In the midst of the crisis on the lake, Jesus responded by doing what the disciples should have done—He stayed in peace and spoke to the wind. They had the promise *we're going to the other side.* Fear and their current circumstances caused them to forget what Jesus had told them. He simply spoke to the storm: "Fully awake, he rebuked the storm and shouted to the sea, 'Hush! Be still!'" (Mark 4:39 TPT). The storm caused the disciples to get into a position of fear, which moved them from the place of trust. Jesus responded by asking them, "Why are you so afraid? Haven't you learned to trust yet?" (verse 40 TPT).

As a next-level believer, fully commit to submitting your thought life to the Holy Spirit. Gain understanding concerning the importance of having a renewed mind. This means your mind is made new. Through your renewed mind, God's original purpose and plan are reactivated in your life.

Application

Fear will inhibit you from seeing yourself as a next-level believer who is anointed to influence your family, community and region for the Kingdom of God. Take a moment and make a list of fears hindering you from seeing yourself the way God sees you. What is blocking your view of your identity? Commit to praying over the list of fears and hindrances daily until each fear or hindrance is no longer an issue.

Powerful Words

Jesus was not limited to acts of healing. He fully walked in dominion over "things" that manifested around Him. He operated in Kingdom power and authority. If someone was sick, Jesus spoke the words "be healed." When Lazarus died, Jesus simply said, "Lazarus, come out!" (John 11:43). He was calling Lazarus to come out from the place of death. When the fig tree failed to produce fruit in the season of fruit bearing, Jesus simply spoke words commanding the tree to die and not bear fruit again (see Matthew 21:19). Jesus showed us the power of words by walking in dominion and authority, just as Adam and Eve had before they sinned in the Garden of Eden.

It is time to use your words to reposition your life and begin walking and living as a next-level believer. It is time for you to come into your destiny, and this begins by coming into agreement with God. In other words, it is time to start saying what you hear God saying.

Don't be limited by what you see. Jesus wasn't. He called those things that were not as though they were (see Romans 4:17). That is the power of prophetic capacity, which we will discuss in chapters 5 and 6. You have been given the supernatural ability to speak words that unlock restoration, shift circumstances and reorder things in the environment around you so that they align with God's intent and purpose. You are more powerful than you give yourself credit for. God has endowed you with supernatural capacity. In our next chapter, we will discuss the Church, the Ekklesia, and how as the Church we must gain greater revelation to begin transforming the gates of society.

Reflection

Consider a specific time when you struggled with embracing the Kingdom power and authority God has given you. Why do you think you struggled in that situation? Make a list of reasons why you found the situation difficult. Be faithful to submit these things on the list to the Lord until they are no longer problematic for you.

Prayer Activation

I confess that I am a speaking spirit made in the image and likeness of God. The power of the Holy Spirit is within me. I have been given power and authority to influence everything around me. Today, I break the covenant of silence that has been blocking my voice. I commit to declaring the Word of God daily. I activate my voice, which is linked to the power and authority I have been given, in Jesus' name.

3

The Ruling Church

And this rock [the truth of who I am] will be the bedrock foundation on which I will build my church—my legislative assembly, and the power of death will not be able to overpower it!

Matthew 16:18 TPT

The Church is called to be the voice of God's Kingdom in the earth. This means we are to represent the Kingdom, advancing God's agenda and using our influence to shift cities, regions and nations. The Church was never designed as a place for believers to gather each week, sit in the pews, sing a few songs, hear a nice sermon and have no Kingdom expression. The Church should consist of radical believers who are so impacted by the supernatural presence of God in the weekly gatherings that they become influencers in their workplace and community.

When I speak of community, I am referring to what is commonly known as the "seven mountains of culture" or "seven mountains of influence." These mountains are government, marriage/family, arts/entertainment, media, religion/church, education and business. We can consider these seven mountains of influence as gates, and I will give definition to each of them later in this chapter. First, however, let's take a closer look at how such gates function.

Understanding Gates

A gate can be defined as a structural closure through a wall, a fence or a barrier for the purpose of transitioning from one place to another. Gates allow people to move from one area into another. They are access points that open the way into something. Another word for gate is *portal*. There are both physical and spiritual gates.

Your physical body has five gates: eyes, ears, touch, taste and smell. More commonly, these five gates are called the senses, but they are also gates. They are access points. When I am in the grocery store, I often walk through the coffee aisle, which is usually pungent with the smell of coffee. Almost immediately, my desire for a cup of coffee is awakened through the gate of my sense of smell. You can find commercials for different products in any form of media, print, social media or television. By accessing your eye gates, these commercials are at work on you, attempting to influence you to buy certain products. Individuals who are bound by addictions such as pornography, drugs and/or alcohol were taken captive through their physical gates. These are just a few examples of how our natural gates are accessed.

Old Testament cities were surrounded by walls and gates. The benefits were that the gates provided protection and a place where government officials could meet to render judicial decisions (see Joshua 2:7; 2 Samuel 18:24; 19:8). The gates were also a place where business and social functions were carried out, where contracts were signed and witnessed, and where prophets could deliver the word of the Lord to the city elders (see Ruth 4:1; Jeremiah 7:1–3). Judicial verdicts were handed down at the gates. Absalom sat at the gate and stole the hearts of many of Israel's leaders from his father, King David (see 2 Samuel 15:2–4).

Gates were places of great strength. When Jesus declared that the gates of hell would not prevail against His Church, He was declaring that the forces of hell would not overcome the Church (see Matthew 16:18). Regardless of the plots, stratagems or strength of Satan and his angels, the Ekklesia will not be overcome. As the Ekklesia, we will face off the kingdom of Satan from generation to generation, but we will not be overcome.

Symbolic of authority and power, gates are mentioned numerous times throughout Scripture. Here are a few examples:

Go through, go through the gates. Prepare the way of the people; build up, build up the highway. Remove the stones; lift up a standard over the peoples (Isaiah 62:10).

Open the gates, that the righteous nation may enter, the one who remains faithful (Isaiah 26:2).

Therefore, your gates shall be open continually; they shall not be shut day nor night, so that men may bring to you the wealth of the nations, and that their kings may be brought (Isaiah 60:11).

Scripture also mentions examples like the *gate of heaven*, *Zion's gate*, and the *gates of righteousness*:

How awesome is this place! This is none other but the house of God, and this is the gate of heaven (Genesis 28:17).

The LORD loves the gates of Zion more than all the dwelling places of Jacob (Psalm 87:2).

Open to me the gates of righteousness; I will go into them, and I will praise the LORD (Psalm 118:19).

Then there are also *evil gates* that Scripture mentions:

I will go before you and make the crooked places straight; I will break in pieces the gates of bronze and shatter the bars of iron (Isaiah 45:2).

Thus says the LORD of Hosts:
"The broad wall of Babylon will be utterly broken, and her high gates will be burned with fire; and the peoples will labor in vain, and the nations become exhausted only for fire" (Jeremiah 51:58).

I will build My church, and the gates of Hades shall not prevail against it (Matthew 16:18).

Following Peter's declaration that Jesus was the Christ, Son of the living God, Jesus declared that the Church would be established on this truth: Christ is the Son of the living God, and through Him we have redemption. *Clarke's Commentary* tells us that when Jesus went on to declare that He would build His Church and that the gates of hell would not overcome it, He was referring to the plots, stratagems and strength of Satan and his kingdom.[1]

The Church has endured great persecution from generation to generation. Yet Jesus declared that the powers and stratagems of Satan's kingdom would not overcome the Church. In every generation, assignments of hell manifest against the Church, with a primary aim of silencing the Church. But the cornerstone of the Church is Christ Himself, who has already won the victory and who cannot be defeated. This is the truth that the Church has been commissioned to declare and demonstrate—the power of Christ's supernatural Kingdom. It is important to remember that the Church is not the Kingdom of God. The Church is a manifestation of the Kingdom, and has been endued with power and authority to overcome the darkness.

Defining the Ekklesia

"And continuing daily with one mind in the temple, and breaking bread from house to house, they ate their food with gladness and simplicity of heart, praising God and having favor with all the people. And the Lord added to the church daily those who were being saved" (Acts 2:46–47).

When Jesus declared His intent to build His Church, He used the word *ekklesia*. This word was not unfamiliar to the disciples, who would have understood the word to embody a foreign stronghold. The same word was also used to describe religious assemblies.[2] The idea of the Church as an ekklesia (assembly or gathering) is taken from common usage, where the word was applied to the "calling out" of citizens for a civic meeting, or of soldiers for battle. The term is used this way in Scripture to refer to the people of God (see Deuteronomy 4:10; 9:10; Acts 5:11; Ephesians 1:22; Hebrews 12:23).[3]

Jesus' use of the term *ekklesia* conveyed an expansion of its meaning to include more than people being called for a secular civic meeting or a natural battle. The Church would now function as the Ekklesia. From the use of the term in this way, the disciples understood that they were being deployed for spiritual legislation that would expand the Kingdom of God.

When Jesus mentioned the Ekklesia, He was not referring to buildings, He was referring to people. He was expressing the purpose of the Church, the Ekklesia, to govern and legislate wherever its people lived. The Ekklesia, therefore, is not a collection of people passively waiting for the end. The Ekklesia is a movement of people who are filled with the supernatural presence of God and committed to influencing their families, workplaces, cities and nations for His Kingdom.

The Ekklesia consists of more than pastors and church leaders. Every believer is included. Those in the Ekklesia understand that through their influence, territorial gains are made for the Kingdom of God. Territorial gains are connected to human, financial and other types of resources that are used to continue the expansion of God's Kingdom. Expansion is growth. God wants the Church to grow, in order that more of the Ekklesia can be deployed. Like a mighty army, members of the Ekklesia are to use their supernatural arsenal to overthrow the forces of hell and to set captives free.

Acts 2:32–47 reveals several characteristics of the New Testament Church, the Ekklesia. I encourage you to study this passage diligently and let the Holy Spirit show you even more characteristics that may not be listed here.

1. *Kingdom message.* Declaring Jesus as Lord and Christ, Peter delivered a clear message to his hearers: Jesus is Lord and Messiah; turn from sin (see Acts 2:32–33, 36–38). The message the Church carries now must likewise be clear: "Jesus is Lord and Messiah; turn from sin." The Church must not submit to the assignment of darkness that is trying to influence her to become silent. There cannot be any compromise. We cannot alter our message to appease political parties, denominational stances or anything else.

2. *Influence.* Peter preached with authority and power, just as Jesus had done. The result was that the hearts of his hearers were "moved," and they were stirred to the

point of action, asking, "What shall we do?" (verse 37).
The Church that Jesus is building walks in authority
and power, as Peter did, which manifest in great influence from generation to generation.

3. *Increase.* Increase and expansion are characteristics
   of the Church. "The same day there were added unto
   them . . ." (verse 41 KJV). The clear message, "Jesus
   is Lord and Messiah; turn from sin," resulted in increase. John 15 commands us to bear fruit. Barrenness is not a characteristic of the Ekklesia. We must
   bear fruit, and our fruit should remain. This includes
   bearing the fruit of the character and nature of
   Christ.

4. *Consistency.* Those who received Christ grew from
   being believers to walking and living as disciples. They
   regularly attended when the apostles were teaching,
   they shared communion from house to house and they
   attended prayer gatherings. The believers in the early
   Church met "constantly" (verse 44 TLB). As a next-level
   believer, you must commit to walking and living as a
   disciple, which is not always convenient, but is always
   necessary.

5. *Fear of the Lord.* "And fear came upon every soul"
   (verse 43 KJV). The fear mentioned here refers to the
   reverential fear and awe of God. *Strong's Concordance* key #5401 cites *Vine's Expository Dictionary
   of New Testament Words*, which explains it this way:
   "Reverential fear . . . of God, as a controlling motive of the life, in matters spiritual and moral, not
   a mere 'fear' of His power and righteous retribution, but a wholesome dread of displeasing Him, a
   'fear' which banishes the terror that shrinks from His
   presence."[4]

6. *Regular worship.* Believers in the early Church were "continuing daily with one mind in the temple" (verse 46). Gathering for corporate worship was an integral part of church life among these believers.

7. *Miracles.* Miracles were common in the early Church. "Many wonders and signs were done through the apostles" (verse 43). As the Church continues to shift into her identity, we will see many more signs and wonders manifest, not just through those who identify as apostles, but also among believers.

8. *Joy and thankfulness.* Believers in the early Church not only gathered daily in the temple, but they also broke bread. They ate their food "with gladness and singleness of heart" (verse 46 KJV).

9. *Favor.* Early Church believers lived "having favor with all the people" (verse 47). I define *favor* as the supernatural force of God operating in our lives. Favor causes unusual doors to open. Blessings manifest as a result of favor (see Esther 2:15; Psalm 45:2; 84:11; Daniel 1:9; Luke 2:52). Kingdom believers operate in great favor.

10. *Giving.* "They sold their property and goods and distributed them to all, according to their need" (verse 45). Kingdom believers are generous in their giving. While all believers do not have the same capacity to give, Kingdom believers are consistent givers.

11. *Unity.* Early Church believers were strengthened and encouraged, and they walked in unity (see verse 42). When unity prevails among us as believers, our influence increases. Division among us hinders our witness and must be resolved.

Application

Spend time reviewing these eleven points and allow the Holy Spirit to speak to you concerning these characteristics in your life. Be faithful to submit to whatever the Holy Spirit shows you. Remember, God helps us surrender to Him.

Different Models, Same Function

From generation to generation, we must cultivate these characteristics we just reviewed in the Church. Without these characteristics, the Church becomes entrenched in formalism and the traditions of man. When this occurs, rather than functioning as the Ekklesia, the Church falls under the influence of culture, and believers stop functioning as influencers of culture for God's Kingdom.

The book of Acts provides powerful descriptions and testimonies of the early Church. Those believers walked in power and authority, using their influence to impact cities, regions and nations. They understood their identity as the Ekklesia and their mandate to impact the world for the Kingdom of God. Even in the midst of difficult times when the Church was being persecuted, its people continued to overcome the darkness of Satan's kingdom. The early Church serves as a model of how the Church should function today.

> Those who gladly received his word were baptized, and that day about three thousand souls were added to them (Acts 2:41).

> And the Lord added to the church daily those who were being saved (Acts 2:47).

> These men who have turned the world upside down have come here also (Acts 17:6).

Culture, Mountains and Influence

In his book *Ekklesia: Rediscovering God's Instrument for Global Transformation*, Ed Silvoso states,

> Back then, church always referred to *people*, never to *buildings*, and it was made up of individuals who operated 24/7 "from house to house," all over town as a transforming organism, not as a static institution. . . . Its objective was the transformation of people *and of society*, rather than acting as a transfer station for saved souls bound for heaven.[5]

The current model of the Church too often focuses on it as a static institution. This is evidenced by an inward focus on the believers who assemble each week, and too often there are no city invasion plans. In chapter 4 we will discuss the need for reformers and reformation. Here, let me say that if the Church is to rule in the gates of culture—if we are going to possess the gates of the enemy—we must return to the model of the early Church. The *Ekklesia* of that time understood the necessity of invasion and turned the whole world upside down.

An objective glance at the seven gates or mountains of culture—government, marriage/family, arts/entertainment, media, religion/church, education and business—informs us that Satan's kingdom is currently the dominant influence. These seven mountains of culture are powerfully influential. Culture refers to the way of life of groups of people, and to the way things are done within connected groups.

Several years ago, sensing that we seemed to be at an impasse in fulfilling the corporate vision and mandate God had given us, I began to examine the culture of the church I lead. I began monthly meetings with my leadership team, and over the process of time we discovered that the problem was not with our vision, but rather, it was with our culture. From those meetings, I began defining culture as *"this is how we do it here."* Again, culture is powerfully influential.

Where there are people, there is culture. Culture can vary from environment to environment. Culture can be articulated verbally. In its core, however, culture is often nonverbal. The actions of those within a certain culture are clues that can help us define that culture. Take high schools, for example. The student handbook might inform parents and students of an anti-bullying policy. Within the campus, however, bullying may be not only present and pervasive but also ignored by those in authority, leading to a culture of campus bullying.

The seven mountains of culture or influence currently do not reflect the Kingdom of God. The mandate of the Ekklesia is to evict darkness from the places where it is seated and enthrone Jesus and His Kingdom. What, specifically, are these seven mountains? Let's define each one.

Government: The influence of government cannot be overstated. The function of government is to create an orderly societal structure that reflects righteousness. Government either restrains evil or enables it to prosper. The kingdom of Satan can be seen when government engages in prideful ambition and unrighteous control over its citizens. Righteousness is more than our personal relationship with God; it is the promotion of godly justice, social equity and fairness.

Education: Through this mountain, either the truth and principles of God or the deception of the enemy are communicated. The control and influence of Satan's kingdom can be seen through the promotion of humanism, sexual perversion, hedonistic living, etc. This is an operation of the antichrist spirit, a manifestation of the kingdom of darkness.

Media: This mountain of influence interprets information through a lens either of good or evil. Currently, many media sources are using fear to manipulate and control. This kind of fear is not an attribute of the Kingdom of God.

Arts/Entertainment: Values and virtues can either be distorted or celebrated through this mountain of influence. We were created for fellowship and communion with God and each other. Anti-God and anti-family values reflect the influence of Satan' kingdom. Those who are gifted to operate in this mountain have been given gifts designed to glorify God and not themselves.

Business: God has given us the power to create wealth. A portion of our financial resources are intended to honor God and not celebrate mankind. The spirit of Mammon currently controls this mountain of influence, which influences us to think that money is our "source" of life and blessings rather than a "resource" necessary in life. God is our source, however. All blessings flow from Him.

Marriage/Family: Families either reflect the values of God's Kingdom or the agenda of Satan's kingdom. The first murder was committed within the family unit. Many parents have surrendered their authority to mold the minds of their children toward morality and righteousness. They have given that authority to schools and the media, which currently reflect Satan's kingdom. Ultimately, when parents surrender their authority, the dominant influence in children's lives then comes from principalities, powers and rulers of darkness that control the culture.

Religion/Church: Man was created for relationship with God. Pure religion influences us to worship God in spirit and in truth. The replacement of biblical truth with the doctrines of men, along with having a form of godliness but denying the power thereof, is a manifestation of Satan's kingdom.

Each generation is responsible to influence these seven mountains of culture. Satan is currently ruling each of these mountains, and the Ekklesia must defeat his rulership and claim territory for the Kingdom of God. Don't forget that the war you and I are engaged in is not against flesh and blood, but against the kingdom of Satan. The Bible describes our struggle against evil as *wrestling* (see Ephesians 6:12). *Strong's Concordance* key #3823 defines *wrestling* this way:

A struggle against someone or something that requires close personal contact . . . (a contest between two in which each endeavors to throw the other, and which is decided when the victor is able to hold his opponent down with his hand upon his neck). The term is transferred to the Christian's struggle with the power of evil.

We cannot prevail in our struggle against the kingdom of Satan at a distance. This up-close, personal struggle against evil requires the supernatural strength of the Holy Spirit. Whether you recognize it or not, you are in the midst of a conflict that will continue throughout the course of your life.

Satan does not intend to release his grip on the kingdoms of this world. He considers these earthly kingdoms to belong to him:

Again, the devil took Him [Jesus] up on a very high mountain and showed Him all the kingdoms of the world and their grandeur, and said to Him, "All these things I will give You if You will fall down and worship me."

Matthew 4:8–9

In exchange for Jesus' worship, Satan offered all the earthly kingdoms to Him. Satan fights to maintain control of this world's systems, and to do so he attacks the hearts, minds and souls of men and women. He blinds the minds of unbelievers to keep them from seeing and receiving the truth of God's love for them. He attacks believers in their prayer life and worship, and in their daily walk, which is connected to their purpose and destiny.

Dear one, your warfare will not end until your life on earth is finished. The Holy Spirit has anointed and empowered you to prevail over the kingdom of Satan. You have been given everything you need to win against the assaults of darkness.

Application

Are there areas of your life where Satan seems to prevail over you? Take time to list each area and submit your list to God in prayer daily. As you see the battle turn and you are walking in victory, take time to honor God and celebrate your victory. God has given you power and authority to war and win over Satan's kingdom.

Characteristics of Ruling Churches

Ruling Churches have a distinct identity and focus. Ruling churches understand their mandate to equip and train believers to do the work of the ministry, according to Ephesians 4:11–13. Ruling churches mobilize and deploy believers as an army that walks in power and authority.

A dimension of the word *power* includes violence. Ruling churches engage in violent prayer and violent worship, relentless in their mandate to overcome and overthrow Satan's kingdom. Ruling churches are not content with the status quo of culture. They use their influence to expand the Kingdom of God, take territory and impact culture. In the next chapter, I will discuss the characteristics and distinctions of Kingdom reformers. These reformers walk in power and authority and are relentless in their mandate to influence culture for the Kingdom of God.

Reflection

Review the descriptions I provided of the seven mountains of influence: government, marriage/family, arts/entertainment, media, religion/church, education and business. Ask the Lord to show you where you are called to have great influence.

Prayer Activation

Lord, I thank You that You have empowered me to overcome the darkness. I confess that I am anointed and empowered to possess the gates of the enemy. Darkness cannot overcome me, but through the power of the Holy Spirit I overcome the darkness, in Jesus' name.

PART 2

Revealing the Reformers

This second section of the book will focus on the Kingdom army and the division of leadership God has positioned in the Church. Reformers have been present on the earth from generation to generation. Who are these reformers? They are the apostles and prophets, but they can also be the believers who are connected and aligned with the apostles and prophets. These Spirit-filled believers who are not called as an apostle or prophet are working as teachers, service people in the marketplace, businessmen and women, mothers and fathers, etc. Mark 16:15–19 tells us that believers are to go into all the world and that signs shall follow them. As these believers cultivate and carry the spirit of reformation into their various spheres of influence, they can do mighty Kingdom deeds. The pattern of the Church in the book of Acts is the foundation for today's Church. All believers are to be equipped to function. When next-level believers function in the roles God has assigned to them, reformation is released.

4

The Era of Apostles and Apostolic Believers

Then Jesus came and spoke to them, saying, "All authority has been given to Me in heaven and on earth. Go therefore and make disciples of all nations, baptizing them in the name of the Father and of the Son and of the Holy Spirit."

Matthew 28:18–19

In every generation, God raises up reformers who are anointed to correct, rectify, reclaim, renovate, recover and deliver in the territories assigned to them. These reformers are apostles who are anointed by God to raise up apostolic believers. We are currently witnessing the rise of more and more apostles who are called for this generation. Reformers have assigned territories that are their sphere of influence, and they are commissioned to exercise Kingdom rule in those territories. Reformers can be found throughout every strata of culture: government, marriage/family, arts/entertainment, media, religion/church, education and business. These reformers are influencers for the Kingdom of God.

The mandate of Kingdom rulership is not limited to those called to the fivefold ministry, however, but includes all believers. As God's reformers work and live in the places where they have been assigned, they manifest the authority and power they have been given. This results in changed lives!

> And he has appointed some with grace to be apostles, and some with grace to be prophets, and some with grace to be evangelists, and some with grace to be pastors, and some with grace to be teachers. And their calling is to nurture and prepare all the holy believers to do their own works of ministry, and as they do this they will enlarge and build up the body of Christ. These grace ministries will function until we all attain oneness into the faith, until we all experience the fullness of what it means to know the Son of God, and finally we become one into a perfect man with the full dimensions of spiritual maturity and fully developed into the abundance of Christ.
>
> Ephesians 4:11–13 TPT

The ministry of a reformer is linked with fulfillment of the Great Commission. Believers are commanded to "go" and make disciples of all nations. This does not mean that you must become a missionary who travels to other countries. There are believers who have been commissioned in this way, yet most believers are not. While you may not be called to preach and influence in other nations, you are commissioned to preach and influence individuals and families wherever you are.

Identifying Reformers

Who are these reformers and why is their ministry vital to fulfilling the Great Commission? From the beginning of time, God has expressed His desire for relationship with the people He has made. In spite of His love and care for mankind throughout time and generations, many people have consistently chosen their own way over God's way. His response to this has been to raise up reformers to whom He makes known His desires and plans. Then He sends these reformers to His people to influence them to return to Him with their whole heart. These reformers are the "sent ones."

This anointing can also be expressed in the terms *apostle* and *apostolic people*. The term *apostle* refers to those called to the fivefold ministry office of an apostle. The term *apostolic people* describes those who are aligned with an apostle, forming an apostolic company or apostolic community that operates strongly in this dimension through impartation.

It is important for the Church to understand the concept of being sent. Luke 9:2 states, "And he sent them to preach the kingdom of God and to heal the sick." We can see here that the disciples were sent. John Eckhardt, who is overseer of Crusader's Ministries in Chicago and has a strong apostolic call himself, said this:

> To be an apostle, or to be apostolic, revolves around the concept of being sent. Only sent ones can fulfill the Great Commission. Only sent ones will be able to overcome the impossible odds that stand in the way of being able to say, "Mission accomplished." The Church cannot succeed without operating strongly in this dimension.[1]

The office of the apostle is one of five leadership gifts Jesus gave to the Church. When apostles are identified and released to operate in the anointing God has given them, those people connected to them operate in a greater measure of grace to preach the Gospel and demonstrate the power of the Kingdom of God. This is the apostolic company of people.

Through the reformer's anointing, the Great Commission can be fulfilled. Without this anointing, the Church becomes legalistic and rigid. Corporate gatherings can become formalized and resistant to the movement of the Holy Spirit. When apostolic grace is present in corporate gatherings, however, believers are activated in their ministry gift and call to disciple communities, cities, regions and nations. Individual believers are empowered to walk in power and authority, releasing the spirit of reformation. You must operate as a sent one.

Defining the Gift of Apostles

The original Greek word translated *apostle* comes from the Greek word *apostolos* and describes one who is sent from one place to another to accomplish a specific mission. David Cannistraci, author and lead pastor of Gateway City Church in San Jose, California, wrote, "Apostles are delegates on a clear mission for an authority figure. They go forth as representatives of their commander, sent to carry out their orders."[2] John Eckhardt expanded on this idea further:

> The word apostle is a word given by the Holy Spirit to describe a particular anointing that is both necessary and beneficial to the church. . . . It was originally a secular term used by the Greeks and Romans to describe special envoys who were sent out for the purpose of establishing the dominion of the empire. These envoys were sent to certain territories and charged to subdue, conquer, convert, instruct, train and establish new subjects in the culture of the empire.[3]

In Matthew 8, we find a revealing encounter between Jesus and a centurion that involves the concept of the term *apostolos*:

> The centurion answered and said, "Lord, I am not worthy that You should come under my roof. But speak the word only, and

my servant will be healed. For I am a man under authority, having soldiers under me. And I say to this man, 'Go,' and he goes, and to another, 'Come,' and he comes, and to my servant, 'Do this,' and he does it."

Verses 8–9

The term *apostolos* was commonly used at that time to describe a commissioned military envoy who was sent to a specific region or territory to bring it under the dominion of the empire. The military envoy was authorized to disciple those who were now captives of the empire.

Application

Consider the definition of apostles as "sent ones." How do you see the anointing of a sent one operating within you? Remember, God gave "some" to be apostles. You might not be called into the office of an apostle, but the nature of a sent one should be evident within your life and ministry.

The Need for Reformation

As in the case of Daniel and his three friends, captives in a new territory were given a new identity and new language (see Daniel 1:1–7). This is a picture of reformation. Thorough instruction in the culture and policies of the kingdom were a matter of routine. Here are some definitions of *reform*:

> To reform means to amend or improve by change of form, or removal of faults or abuses. To reform means to improve, make better, change, remake, renovate, rectify or correct.[4]

> To reform means to reconstitute the life of an individual or nation and bring it into line with a moral or spiritual standard.

The biggest grouping of reform stories in the Bible involves restoring the true worship of God after a nation has embraced idolatry.[5]

We can see reform and the need for reformation throughout history. Some historic reform efforts have involved women's voting rights, child labor, abolition and temperance.[6] It is important to note that not all reform results in renewed spirituality and faith in God. Abortion law reform is an example of reform that violates God's order. It is a manifestation of the kingdom of Satan. Abortion is a modern version of child sacrifice, the shedding of innocent blood. It defiles the land and dishonors God. Child sacrifice was a pagan practice often associated with idolatry among heathen nations. Israel was prohibited from participating in it (see Leviticus 18:21; 1 Kings 12:26–31; 2 Kings 23:10). The spiritual reality of such a law releases a curse upon the land, as the voice of the aborted unborn children's blood cries out to God for justice.

Proverbs 14:34 states, "Righteousness exalts a nation, but sin is a reproach to any people." Nations that choose righteousness are exalted and experience the blessing and favor of God. "Blessed and prosperous is that nation who has God as their Lord! They will be the people he has chosen for his own" (Psalm 33:12 TPT). We are in a season where nations are choosing whether or not they will align with God's Kingdom (see Proverbs 16:2; 21:2; Matthew 25:32; Acts 14:14–17). Although a nation may not choose God as a whole, there will be a righteous remnant in the territory who will choose God's way.

We are in an era when reformers are arising. God uses the voice of reformers, His sent ones, to remind people of His Word. These sent ones are unrelenting in their pursuit of righteousness and their desire to see the Kingdom of God released in great measures so that the Great Commission can be fulfilled. Reformers carry regions and nations in their hearts. In every generation, reformers who understand that they have been sent must arise. God has not changed His mind or His plan, and His plan includes you. The current global crisis signals a need for reformers. Abortion laws must be repealed, and the rights of unborn children must be protected. The definition of marriage and family must return to biblical order. Arts, entertainment and media must be reformed to the degree that God's order of righteousness is portrayed rather than violence and perversion. Education can no longer be used as a gate of access to indoctrinate children into perversion and wickedness. Political corruption is seemingly becoming the norm. Righteous rulers must be elected, and those who would dismiss God as irrelevant in the chambers of government must be sent home. The protests of 2020 were a cry for justice, equity and fairness. Demons and dark powers fueled media misinformation campaigns designed to create fear and division. Into this scenario, reformers must arise. Without reformers, darkness will continue to increase. Dear one, you cannot remain content to sit on the sidelines as a spiritual spectator. You are anointed as a Kingdom influencer. It is time to take your place.

Reformers in Scripture

Reformers are anointed to release a clear word of the Lord and to demonstrate the power of God. We can see the pattern of reformers and reformation throughout Scripture. Here are some examples:

- Ezra—marriage reform regarding intermarriage with pagans (see Ezra 10:1–15).
- Nehemiah—worship and marriage reform continued (see Nehemiah 13).

- Josiah—Judah rediscovered the law of God, resulting in worship reform (see 2 Kings 22–23).

- Barnabas and Paul—ministered as a team, establishing churches (see Acts 13:1–3).

- Tychicus—was described as an able minister (see Ephesians 6:21–22).

Reformers are sent ones. Jesus, the perfect apostle, fully modeled the ministry anointing of a sent one. Throughout Scripture, He referred to Himself as having been sent by the Father (see Matthew 10:40; 15:24; Mark 9:37; Luke 4:18–19, 43; 10:16; John 5:30; 7:16, 29). Jesus challenged false teachings and gave correct interpretation of Scripture (see Matthew 5–7). He challenged religious structures, hypocrisy and corruption. There is no greater apostle than Jesus.

We are in an era of the ministry of the reformers. God is revealing His sent ones who will represent righteousness and be a voice against unrighteousness. Territories and nations are in a time of choosing (see Matthew 25:32). We can either choose to align with God's order and come under the authority of the Kingdom of God, or by default we choose the kingdom of Satan. Neutrality is not an option. God has a plan! The Church must embrace her identity as a ruling voice in the earth and forego the pursuit of cultural and political acceptance at the expense of neutralizing her voice. The apostolic company resists the seduction to become secularized. You must embrace your identity as an influencer in the earth by continually committing to God's agenda.

When the apostolic anointing is the dominant anointing in the Church, believers will walk in the anointing of sent ones, forming a powerful apostolic company. This powerful company overcomes the lure of darkness that would, in essence, silence their voices. As an example, eunuchs were common in the Old

Testament and were often assigned to serve in the king's palace. Subjected to castration, they were unable to produce children. Another way to look at this is that they lacked the capacity to produce the future. There was no reproductive capacity within them. This is a form of silencing.

In the Old Testament, God sent some prophets like Samuel, Nathan, Elijah, Isaiah and Daniel to prophesy to kings. When He wanted to convey His message to a particular king over Israel, He would send a prophet. Yet there were also false prophets who prophesied according to the will of the king. The king controlled their voices. Such false prophets, along with the eunuchs, were supported by the king. In other words, they ate from the king's table (see 1 Kings 18:19).

Apostolic reformers refuse to compromise. They will neither be silenced nor controlled by others. Not only do they build for the current time; they also build for the future. This is a picture of a legacy. Not every believer is called to the office of an apostle. Yet believers will carry the anointing of such a sent one and will manifest great Kingdom influence as a result of their alignment with apostles.

How are you aligned? Are you connected to an apostolic company? Within an apostolic company, believers are equipped and trained to do the work of ministry. Ephesians 4:11–16 provides us with an understanding of the role of church government, which includes those in the fivefold offices equipping believers to do the work of ministry. The process of equipping includes helping believers understand their purpose and identity, in order that they will become fully functional as the Ekklesia.

Reformers are God's supernatural influencers who provoke fallen people to return to God. As apostolic reformer C. Peter Wagner wrote, "Every generation needs apostles to bring a fresh approach to ministry. They discover and restore truths and ministries that have been hidden or have been dormant within the Church."[7] The Church must return to her Kingdom mandate. You have been given power and authority. When you are silent, Satan's kingdom exerts its influence and people are held captive in darkness. But when you walk in the power and authority God has given you, you are influencing those around you for the Kingdom of God.

Distinctions of Reformers

Reformers have been present in God's affairs from the beginning and are present in every generation. Reformers are not only those who are called to function in fivefold ministry as apostles, prophets, pastors, teachers and evangelists. All believers are called as reformers, delivering people from bondage and bringing them into the Kingdom of God. Reformers are fearless and committed individuals. Filled with vision and purpose, reformers are tenacious, unrelenting in fulfilling the purpose for which they have been sent. Here are some of the primary distinctions that set reformers apart:

- *Love.* Reformers have a love for the people and the territory they are called to.
- *Prayer.* Reformers carry themselves and the people they are called to in prayer.
- *Revelation.* Reformers access heaven's blueprints and strategies through prayer.
- *Favor.* Reformers walk in supernatural favor.
- *Persecution.* Reformers attract attacks because of their anointing.
- *Anointing.* Reformers have an anointing to mobilize the Kingdom workforce assigned to them. Reformers build with a team.

- *Restorers.* Reformers are called to restore what has been broken down.

- *Challengers of religious mindsets.* Reformers break through the religious structures holding unbelievers in darkness and also bring the Church back to a Kingdom mentality.

- *Encouragers.* Reformers encourage believers to walk in power and authority.

- *Worship.* Reformers are committed to God's Kingdom pattern of worship.

- *Courage.* Reformers are not afraid to confront wickedness.

- *Harvest mentality.* Reformers are focused on fulfilling the Great Commission by taking territory through gathering the harvest of souls.

- *Faith.* Reformers operate in great faith.

- *Grace.* Reformers operate in great grace.

- *Spiritual warfare.* Reformers know how to labor with heaven to overcome the kingdom of Satan.

- *Influencers.* Reformers have supernatural capacity to influence people to turn to God.

- *Wisdom.* Reformers walk in supernatural wisdom.

Whenever God initiates something new, He identifies a person in a place and gives that person His plan. Such individuals are reformers. God has identified you to stand in the land as a powerful representative of the Kingdom of God. You have everything you need to fulfill God's plan. Everyone in your sphere of authority is waiting for you to arise and shift to the next level. As you do so, you will impact their lives for change.

Reflection

Consider the list you just read of the distinctions of reformers. Which of these characteristics are strongest within you? Which are weaker? Create a list of your weaker characteristics and present them to the Lord. Begin to watch for ways in which the Holy Spirit is developing these characteristics in your life. Take time daily to decree prophetically that these characteristics are coming alive within you.

Prayer Activation

Lord, thank You for the power of reformation that You have placed upon my life. I confess that I am a reformer, filled with power and authority. I am part of a powerful apostolic company that You have raised up for this time. You have given to me a measure of grace sufficient enough to accomplish Your will. I decree that I am increasing more and more, in Jesus' name.

5

The Era of the Prophetic Company

> God has put these in the church: first apostles, second prophets . . .
>
> 1 Corinthians 12:28

What is the role of prophets and prophetic people in advancing the mandate of heaven through fulfillment of the Great Commission? In every generation, God has used prophets and prophecy to carry His message. He uses prophets and prophecy to call people to repentance, to warn of impending judgment and to declare His intent. Like the office of an apostle, the office of a prophet is a leadership gift given to the Church. Along with apostles, prophets are governmental gifts God has given the Church for equipping believers and for Kingdom advancement. Throughout the New Testament, we find apostles and prophets forming teams to advance the

Kingdom by planting churches and strengthening believers in understanding God's eternal purposes. Along with evangelists, pastors and teachers, God uses these governmental gifts of apostles and prophets to equip believers to do the work of the ministry.

Prophets have the supernatural capacity to identify and activate believers into their Kingdom call. Prophets and prophetic people are an integral part of God's plan. Through prophecy, God calls the nations back to the pattern of worship and warns of error. He has used prophecy to awaken fallen people and to encourage them to return to Him.

Through God's divine call and purpose, prophets and prophetic people are positioned throughout the seven mountains of culture for Kingdom advancement and territorial gains. As these believers access revelation and creativity, they gain supernatural strategies from heaven to overthrow the rulership of darkness operating in their territory. This is reformation.

> He gave some to be apostles, prophets, evangelists, pastors, and teachers, for the equipping of the saints, for the work of service, and for the building up of the body of Christ, until we all come into the unity of the faith and of the knowledge of the Son of God, into a complete man, to the measure of the stature of the fullness of Christ.
>
> Ephesians 4:11–13

Ignorance about the Prophetic

Prophecy and prophets still remain largely misunderstood. Teaching materials and conferences concerning the prophetic continue to increase, yet misunderstanding concerning this valuable gift remains. The influence of religious traditions and the philosophies of those who continue to teach cessationism fosters ignorance around prophets and prophetic people. Cessationism is a theological teaching that denies the continuance of apostles and prophets after the death of the twelve apostles, along with Paul. This doctrine also teaches that the charismatic gifts of the Spirit (see 1 Corinthians 13:8–10) ceased in the first century and were replaced by the canon of the New Testament Scriptures.[1] Today, Bible colleges tend to ignore the important subject of the gifts of the Spirit, placing greater emphasis on other theological issues, including cessationism.

As a Bible teacher and pastor, I understand the importance of exegetical accuracy. An overemphasis on the letter of the Word of God, however, without equal emphasis on the spiritual manifestation and outworking of the Word, can create an imbalance. This imbalance leads to legalism, which is a religious spirit that focuses on rule keeping. This is an old wineskin that too often denies the power of the Spirit. "They may pretend to have a respect for God, but in reality they want nothing to do with God's power" (2 Timothy 3:5 TPT). Old wineskins are rigid and inflexible. They are incapable of holding new wine (see Matthew 9:17). New wine is a reference to revelation. While there are truths that do not change from generation to generation, such as sanctification, justification and redemption through the blood of Jesus, there are other things you must gain revelation about, such as the power of the Holy Spirit, harvest strategies and how to use the gifts of the Spirit, which are still relevant today and must be embraced.

God's intent was not for you or me to be a pew sitter. God did not design our corporate gatherings to be Christian entertainment. Our gatherings are for powerful preaching and teaching, prophecy, healing and miracles, resulting in a harvest of souls. When you are trained and activated in the gifts of the Spirit and are released in the corporate gatherings to minister to other believers there, it builds your faith so that you realize you can also operate in the gifts outside the corporate gatherings, influencing those around you for the Kingdom of God. This is what the spirit of reformation looks like.

Believers need sound theological doctrine, as well as training and activation in spiritual operations, including prophecy. The apostle Paul encouraged believers to prophesy: "I desire that you all speak in tongues, but even more that you prophesy" (1 Corinthians 14:5). Prophesy was an integral part of the New Testament believers' lives. If the Church is to fulfill the Great Commission, we must understand the role of prophecy. You must be trained, activated and encouraged to prophesy. As author, apostolic leader and pastor Paula Price has written,

> People, because of information and education neglect, just do not grasp the significance of the office and its usefulness to God. Therefore, those called to the prophetic are too often unskilled in its functions; making many who encounter them shun God's prophets as a result.[2]

As I said earlier, a lack of understanding of spiritual things is ignorance. Prophecy is revelatory in nature and must be embraced. Given the biblical emphasis on operating in the gifts of the Spirit, particularly prophecy, Kingdom influencers should understand how to use prophecy as both a gift and a weapon that pushes back darkness. When you use it in these ways, you reveal the Father's heart.

Application

What do you believe about prophets and prophecy? Write your theology concerning this in your journal. Once you are finished, compare what you believe to what the Bible says. Be committed to submit your opinion to the Lord and allow Him to adjust your theology where your theology is in need of correction.

Prophetic Reformers

To *reform* means to make changes in something (typically a social, political, or economic institution or practice) in order to improve it. A few other words that describe reform are *renovate*, *reorient*, *rectify* or *correct*, *reshape*, *remake*, *rebuild* and *change*. The sixteenth century was a notable period of reformation. Martin Luther, a German monk, wrote ninety-five theoretical questions protesting the practices of clergy abuse, greed, corruption and faulty doctrine within the Catholic Church. Martin Luther's protests of the Catholic Church's practices and inconsistencies in doctrine led to a split of the Church and the formation of the Protestant Church.

Similarly, each generation must carry the spirit of reformation. This means that every generation is assigned to release the power and authority of the Kingdom of God to overturn the darkness. You and I must carry the spirit of reformation in our generation. The essential characteristic of reformation is truth. As truth is revealed to you, truth can be revealed through you.

Reformers receive their message from God, who is Truth. As Jesus said in John 14:6, "I am the way, the truth, and the life. No one comes to the Father except through Me." The Kingdom message is a divine message of truth from God to humanity. When that message of truth penetrates the hearts of men and women, it opens their eyes to God's love for them. It is at this moment that they can turn from darkness. Satan uses lies and deception to hold people in darkness, but believers who carry the spirit of reformation have the supernatural capacity to deliver the captives the enemy is holding.

I want to emphasize again that reformers are not limited to those who are called as apostles, prophets, evangelists, pastors and teachers. All believers who understand their identity as the Ekklesia carry the spirit of reformation and are committed to speaking the truth of God as they challenge and push back the darkness. Take a moment now and decree aloud, *I am a reformer!*

Remember, everything in the earthly realm is voice activated. Prophets are reformers, and God uses prophets to vocalize His will and intent. Like apostles, prophets carry a message of repentance that urges men and women to return to God. God uses prophets to vocalize revelation and convey His instructions. This is a picture of illumination. In chapter 3, we discussed the fact that prophets delivered messages from God at the gate of the city. Words of prophecy are powerful. They are like a hammer smashing demonic mindsets and dark agendas. Whenever prophets and prophetic people prophesy, the earth responds. God uses prophecy because He loves the nations. Cities and regions can be delivered from darkness through prophecy.

Glory Reformation

I believe we can draw strength and meaning from this prophecy spoken over the inhabitants of Jerusalem in Isaiah 60:1–3 (AMP):

> Arise [from spiritual depression to a new life], shine [be radiant with the glory and brilliance of the LORD]; for you light has come, and the glory and brilliance of the LORD has risen upon you.
>
> For in fact, darkness will cover the earth and deep darkness will cover the peoples; but the LORD will rise upon you [Jerusalem] and His glory and brilliance will be seen on you.
>
> Nations will come to your light, and kings to the brightness of your rising.

In this era of a pandemic health crisis, economic crisis, escalating violence and confusion, many people have become depressed. Feelings of hopelessness have captured many as they struggle to make sense of the horrific events that continue to unfold. Perhaps you have found yourself in a similar position. God has promised that no matter how dark the darkness, His light will arise and His glory will be seen upon His people. In 2019, the Lord spoke this prophetic word to me: *I am raising up glory hubs. These hubs will radiate My glory in new ways.* When the pandemic of 2020 began, the Lord brought this word back to me and said, *I did not send the pandemic, but I will use it for My purposes. This is the season that you will see the manifestation of glory houses.*

As the Lord spoke, I could see gold and red flames of fire around the earth. I asked Him, *What are the lights?*

The Lord said, *These are the glory houses that I am raising up around the world.*

During the pandemic crisis, people were awakened to prayer and worship in a significant way. Once again, the home became the meeting place to host God's presence. The family altar, which had been abandoned in many homes, was rebuilt, and the fire on the altar was rekindled. Fire represents purification and passion. As a result, the glory of the Lord came down. In the midst of a global crisis, believers were being restored, revived and refreshed. Church attendance was restricted. Instead, worship gatherings were held at places like the beach. People stood on balconies or knelt in front of their homes and sang praises to the Lord.

Through all of this, unbelievers were gaining understanding that God had not abandoned them. In the midst of the crisis, many surrendered their lives to the Lord. One of the greatest harvest seasons was unlocked as the army of the Ekklesia was being reset and positioned for next-level warfare against the enemies of God. Reformation was beginning.

The manifestation of God's glory will result in great harvest. Let me say again, we have entered the greatest harvest season since the beginning of the Church. Nations are coming to our light and to the brightness of our rising. Many prophets and prophetic people have been declaring this word. Whenever God is initiating something new in the earth, He reveals it to His prophets and prophetic people. "Surely the Lord GOD does nothing without revealing His purpose to His servants the prophets" (Amos 3:7). God prepares a people in a given place to reveal and carry His purpose. These are the Ekklesia, modern-day reformers who speak forth God's Word. Ordinary people like you and me, who are filled up with the power of God, will influence cultures for the Kingdom of God.

God is revealing prophets and prophetic people who are committed to carrying the message He has given them. "Therefore also the wisdom of God said, 'I will send them prophets and apostles, and some of them they will kill and persecute'" (Luke 11:49). God is faithful to reveal His eternal plans to prophetic people so that we can align with Him and execute those plans. Just as God is revealing glory hubs, those who have been in the place of intimacy with God are also being revealed. These are prophets who, like John, have put their head on the Lord's chest and have heard his heartbeat. From His heartbeat, they prophesy.

The Issue of Inaccurate Prophesies

All believers should prophesy. Paul, the apostle, desired that all believers would do so: "My preference would be for you all to prophesy by the Spirit. Those who speak prophetically are God's mouthpiece" (1 Corinthians 14:5 VOICE). Prophecy should be an integral characteristic of all believers. Prophecy should be released in our corporate gatherings, and believers should be trained and activated to prophesy. Corporate gatherings should regularly host prophetic training classes that provide sound biblical teaching regarding prophecy.

Beyond the training, opportunity should be given for believers to prophesy in corporate gatherings. If you are a pastor or ministry leader, I encourage you to host mature apostles and prophets who can help you establish the prophetic dimension in your ministry. Don't be afraid of the prophetic messes that will happen. Those prophetic people aligned with you will need time to grow and develop in their prophetic grace and call. "Let all things be done in decency and in order," says 1 Corinthians 14:40. We have often majored on "decency and in order," and have not created opportunity for "let all things be done." It is time for believers to embrace their prophetic identity. It is time for you to embrace and grow in your prophetic identity.

An important aspect of prophetic training is the development of a prophetic protocol and the creation of a "safe place" for believers to grow and develop. This safe place facilitates the establishment of prophetic communities. Isolated prophets are at risk for prophetic error since there is no accountability structure surrounding them. I will talk more specifically about prophetic protocol at the end of this chapter, but for now, if you are leading a ministry, consider this question: How will you handle errors? You must consider this as you develop a prophetic protocol. If you are not leading a ministry but you prophesy, what is your accountability structure? Whom are your life and ministry submitted to?

I have had opportunity to speak with people who became discouraged because a prophecy did not come to pass. During the 2020 elections in the United States, a significant number of prophecies concerning who would be elected was released. Prophecies were regularly shared on social media platforms. Unfortunately, many of these prophecies did not manifest. My use of the term *unfortunate* here is not based on the election outcomes, which were different than the majority of prophecies I heard. I am using this term to describe the aftermath. I wondered how credible prophets had erred concerning this issue. How could so many credible prophets be wrong?

As I pondered this issue, I considered the prophet Micaiah, whose story we find in 1 Kings 22. In Micaiah's story you will find several principles that can help you enlarge your capacity as a prophetic reformer. Two kings, Ahab and Jehoshaphat, formed a partnership to reclaim territory that King Ahab had lost in a previous war. King Jehoshaphat suggested that prior to going to war, they should ask the word of the Lord. In other words, King Jehoshaphat suggested that they receive prophetic ministry, saying, "Please ask for a word from the LORD today" (1 Kings 22:5).

Prophetic ministry gives you access to God's intentions. King Jehoshaphat determined that God's opinion regarding their collaborative war effort was important. Heeding his advice, King Ahab convened a prophetic gathering with four hundred prophets and asked whether or not he should go to war. The response was a resounding *yes*. Each prophet declared that King Ahab would defeat the enemy and reclaim the territory he had previously lost in battle. Without dissent, these four hundred prophets declared, "Yes, because the LORD will let you defeat Ramoth Gilead" (1 Kings 22:6 ERV). Their prophetic counsel could not have been more incorrect. There is much we can learn about prophetic issues from this story.

Beware of These Issues

Beware of the prophetic error of conformity because someone you respect prophesied a particular event. I have often noted in prophetic gatherings that when one prophet releases a word in a particular vein, all of the prophets will coalesce around that same word. This happened in the story about Micaiah we are looking at, and it is particularly true of believers who are new to prophetic ministry and are developing their prophetic voice. They often lack confidence in their ability to hear an accurate word of the Lord themselves and will remain in the same vein as those around them. I am not advocating for prophetic confusion, which is caused by every prophetic believer prophesying something radically different in a gathering. What I am saying is that we prophesy by faith, and God will reveal different aspects of the revelation being released. We hear the word of the Lord, and by faith we declare what we hear. Some years ago, God visited several prophets in my church in their dreams. Their dreams occurred on the same night. A few days later, when they arrived at the corporate gathering, they each shared the dream they had been given. They had each been given different parts of the same dream. Like a puzzle, each dreamer's dream fit into place, forming the prophetic tapestry of a message from God.

Beware of not accurately judging prophecy. The four hundred prophets in 1 Kings 22 all prophesied the same word: *You will defeat your enemies.* This is an example of how error can occur. Each prophet simply was saying what the prophet before him had said. Jehoshaphat's response was, "Is there not a prophet of the LORD here whom we can ask?" (verse 7). It is interesting to note the distinction these passages make. The four hundred prophets were not identified as being "the Lord's prophets." Not all prophets speak for God. Prophecy must be discerned and judged. I believe that this is what King Jehoshaphat did.

Beware of the fear of man. Prophets and prophetic believers must not allow their words to be controlled by people. This does not negate your responsibility to observe prophetic protocol. What I am saying is that you must not operate out of the spirit of fear of man or out of a desire for people's accolades. This would be a manifestation of the spirit of pride, and God resists the proud (see James 4:6). When you operate out of pride and fear of others, this can result in inaccurate prophecies. You must walk in humility, and your heart must remain pure before God. You must commit to speaking only God's words.

Beware of prophetic theatrics. These four hundred prophets prophesied victory. They demonstrated the prophetic word by using horns of iron to depict the enemies being pushed back until Jehoshaphat and Ahab had consumed them (see 1 Kings 22:11). No amount of prophetic theatrics would change the outcome, however, because a lying spirit had been released. The prophets were the deliverers of a prophecy that was wrong.

Beware of the spirit of control. The king's servant sent to find Micaiah instructed him not to deviate from the prophetic word of victory. He informed Micaiah concerning the unanimous prophecy the four hundred prophets had delivered— that the king would win the war—and told Micaiah that he should speak only good and come into agreement with them (see 1 Kings 22:13). Imagine the pressure Micaiah might have experienced as he stood in the gate among four hundred prophets, two kings and the other leaders who may have been present. I am sure he felt overwhelming pressure to conform and just agree. Ahab had described Micaiah as a prophet he hated, saying, "He never prophesies good for me, but always evil" (verse 8). At first, Micaiah did deliver the same prophetic word as all the rest, "Go and prosper, for the LORD will deliver it into the hand of the king" (verse 15). But Ahab knew it was a deviation from the kind of prophecies Micaiah had previously delivered. The king immediately discerned that this prophet had not delivered the word of the Lord to him. Prophetic people must resist ungodly agreements with inaccurate prophecies. This is a form of deception. In this instance, the prophetic word was being delivered to governmental leaders. As I mentioned before, fear of man can lead to prophetic inaccuracy. You must resist the urge to align with the status quo, and you must be willing to stand alone, knowing that you have heard from God and that you will only speak what He has spoken. While you might experience fear and feelings of isolation because the word you delivered was different from everyone else, God's blessings will be upon you because you did not compromise.

Beware of criticism from "religious" prophets who prophesy smooth words to curry favor with kings. King Ahab's response was to rebuke Micaiah: "How many times must I admonish you to tell me only the truth in the name of the Lord?" (1 Kings 22:16). It is at this point that Micaiah declared the word of the Lord that defeat and not victory would be the result of the battle. He was declaring to Ahab that God was not with him and that not only would Ahab be defeated, but he would also lose his life in battle. Micaiah was sent to tell Ahab that he would lose both his life and his kingdom in this war. That is a difficult prophecy to deliver. Sometimes we are sent with difficult words to declare. Nonetheless, the word must be delivered in love and accuracy. Micaiah did just that. The response of the other prophets was to hit and mock him (see verse 24). Ahab's response was to sentence him to prison and order that he be served only bread and water until the king himself returned from war (see verse 27). Here we can see Ahab's rejection of the prophetic word. This was a form of prophet shaming. Sometimes the word you are sent to deliver might be rejected. Remember, you are a prophetic reformer sent to deliver a message on God's behalf. Do not compromise, no matter how difficult it seems.

Looking back at the 2020 election in the United States, considerable prophecy was given. I am not implying that those who prophesied were false prophets. Many of those prophets were trusted and mature prophets in whom I have great confidence. Is it possible that one prophet influenced another? How could so many prophecies be incorrect? I don't have the answers. What I do know is that the enemy has seized an opportunity to try to discredit the prophetic movement. The enemy hates prophetic people and works to silence or discredit their voices.

Silencing the Prophetic Movement

There is a diabolical assignment to silence the voices of prophets and prophetic people. This is not a new assignment. Throughout biblical history, prophets have been attacked because of their words (see 1 Kings 18; Matthew 23:31; Luke 11:47; 1 Thessalonians 2:15). Prophecy is revelatory in nature. Without prophecy, there is not revelation from God about His intentions. "For the testimony of Jesus is the spirit of prophecy" (Revelation 19:10). It is important to say here, of course, that prophecy does not replace or contradict the Bible. God anoints the voices of prophets and prophetic people to declare His Word. Their words carry a call to repentance and reformation. But the message of prophets is not always welcomed and is often received with hostility. In ancient biblical times, prophets like Jeremiah and Micaiah were imprisoned because of their message. Yet there are also individuals and nations like Nineveh who will hear the prophetic message and repent and return to God (see Jonah 3:4–5).

Following the elections, I spoke to an associate who happened to be from another nation. During the conversation, the issue of the election prophecies was raised. She shared stories of similar incidents that had occurred in her nation, where election prophecies that a particular candidate would win did not come to pass. She recounted how many leaders in her nation had become discouraged concerning prophets and prophetic people as a result. This discouragement further resulted in a refusal to receive this vital and necessary ministry in the future. No allowance was made for the growth and development of the gift. Their discouragement resulted in the continuance of religious structures holding the nation captive. Prophetic error or prophetic inaccuracy can lead to disbelief and discouragement.

Here in America, we witnessed a phenomenon that has become termed as *prophet shaming*. Unbelievers rebuked and scoffed at the prophets. Even Christian leaders, some of whom are considered "prophetic leaders" themselves, also called for apologies from those prophets and prophetic people who had "missed it" with the elections. It appeared from all this that we were "throwing the baby out with the bathwater."

How do we handle inaccurate prophecies? They create chaos and confusion, which is not God's intent. He uses prophets and prophecy to reveal His plans and to bless, encourage and correct people. Satan uses prophetic inaccuracy not only to create chaos and confusion, but also to create fear and disbelief. Since he cannot silence the voice of God's prophets, Satan wants to discredit prophecy. Centuries of error, misinterpretation and manipulation fuel disbelief and hostility. Years of abusive cults and irrational prophetic movements have left scars on too many people, the result of which is the continued disbelief of prophecy.[3] At the core of this chaos is an attempt to silence the voice of prophets and prophetic people.

I concur with Christian leaders who say that we must "judge" prophecy and develop a system of prophetic accountability. What happens, however, when the inaccurate prophecy is given by those who are fathers and mothers of the prophetic movement? Their ministries have been proven over time and are marked by maturity and accuracy. Should they be disavowed by the Body of Christ because of an inaccuracy? Should we respond by ending the practice of publicizing prophecy?

The answer is no. We cannot afford to become like the angry mob who chose Barabbas over Jesus, of whom they shouted, "Crucify Him!" Prophecies should be judged. Inaccurate prophecies should be acknowledged. I recommend that prophecies with national and international impact be submitted to trusted, mature prophetic leaders in the Body of Christ before being released.

The Dark Ages were a time in Church history when prophecy was no longer common in the Church. Prophecy was replaced by a religious spirit and the philosophies of men. Tremendous advancement has come through prophecy and the prophetic movement. We need prophetic reformers. If the kingdom of Satan were ever successful in silencing the voice of prophets and prophetic people, the only voice mankind would hear would have its source in the darkness.

As I said, there is great need for prophetic training in the Body of Christ. Through training and activations, believers can gain understanding of why they must prophesy and how to guard and protect their hearts. Your motive while operating prophetically must be love and a desire to see the Kingdom of God advance. Sadly, this is not always the motive of prophets and prophetic people. There are prophetic pitfalls that we must discern, identify and avoid. Those in error must be corrected. When prophecy is not correctly judged, error persists, resulting in much damage. Paula Price has written,

> Faulty or prophetic words would number in the tens of thousands. Homes and businesses have been recklessly sold, dangerous or unprofitable marriages or covenants have been foolishly entered into. Friends and family have parted, and yes, even lives have been lost to the errors of unskilled, unscrupulous, untaught, prophets. Fortunes were lost, lives ruined, and tragedies experienced in the name of the word of the Lord or thus says the Lord.[4]

In spite of this, we must continue to receive and release the word of the Lord.

One characteristic of reformers is their voice. Like a sharp instrument, you must develop prophetic accuracy. It develops over time, as you prophesy. You are a reformer who is called to deliver God's message. Your spiritual senses are exercised by reason of use (see Hebrews 5:14). Your level of accuracy increases as you develop prophetically. Remember that mistakes can happen. Surround yourself with credible leaders who will hold you accountable, and keep growing. Prophetic reformers are vital to helping the Church return to the prophetic path God has purposed for us.

Satan is a deceiver and the father of lies. His goal is to deceive the nations and silence the voice of the Church. Factions, violence, immorality, covenant-breaking and the religious traditions of men are weapons Satan uses to neutralize the Church. Prophets and prophetic people who know that they are reformers are the response of God to the kingdom of darkness. The ministry of the prophet is a key gift for this season. We cannot fully advance the Kingdom without the prophetic. Prophecy has been the catalyst to saving nations, shifting entire regions and changing the course of the Church.

Words are creative. When you speak, the environment around you responds because everything in the earth realm has ears. We see this truth when Jesus spoke to the fig tree. When He said to it, "Let no fruit ever grow on you again," that is what happened (Matthew 21:18–20). Our words are powerfully creative. God's eternal plans are revealed when we prophesy. The prophetic word has power to set in order, confirm, encourage, correct, initiate, activate, comfort and release. Many things will not be released until someone prophesies. God uses His reformers to declare His will and purposes.

Characteristics of Prophetic Reformers

One of the goals of reformation is restoration. When God created Adam and Eve, He placed them in the Garden and gave them rulership. They were responsible to take care of the Garden, reproduce, multiply and subdue everything in the earth. Unfortunately, they surrendered their authority to Satan through their disobedience to God.

Dear one, whenever you surrender an area of your life to the kingdom of darkness, you are surrendering a portion of your power and authority. It is time for you to recover everything the enemy has stolen from you, including your prophetic voice. Even if you have never prophesied, the enemy is working to keep you ignorant concerning the power of your prophetic voice. You must commit to prophetic development so that you gain the necessary revelation to function fully as a reformer. Here are some key characteristics of prophetic reformers:

- Prophetic reformers operate in the prophetic realm. The prophetic realm is supernatural.

- Prophetic reformers are committed to God's agenda and are committed to developing worship and Word-centered lives through worship, prayer and study of God's Word. This is intimacy with God. Intimacy enlarges our capacity to discern His voice.

- Prophetic reformers are tuned to the frequency of God's voice. They hear and understand the counsel and mind of God because they recognize His voice.

- Prophetic reformers are not moved by current events, because their relationship with God anchors them. They do not allow popular trends, world news or other life events in the world to destabilize them.

- Prophetic reformers endeavor to remain relevant to the generation they are called to serve.

- Prophetic reformers are stable in God's unshakeable Kingdom.

- Prophetic reformers discern times and seasons. They are committed to hearing and declaring a now-and-future word of the Lord that will shift nations.

A Matter of Protocol

Earlier in this chapter, I mentioned the need for a prophetic protocol. What do I mean by protocol? One definition of *protocol* is an official set of rules for what actions we should take in a certain situation. It is important for leaders in the Church to govern the flow of corporate gatherings. First Corinthians 14:40 says, "Let all things be done decently and in order." Order is the opposite of confusion. Order is linked with process and procedure. As I said earlier, however, I have found that ministries tend to focus on "decently and in order" while omitting "let all things be done." Prophetic protocol creates the opportunity for ministries to experience the fullest aspect of letting all things be done decently and in order.

One aspect of my ministry is prophetic training and activation through conducting Schools of the Prophets. Many Schools of the Prophets models have been established over the past years. I am referring here to a process of equipping and training believers to hear the voice of the Lord and deliver His message. The schools I am involved with include the prophetic song, along with other aspects of prophetic ministry. I also refer to this model as prophetic activations. Such training facilitates moving believers from a passive role of spectatorship, wherein they watch others do the work of the ministry, to becoming activated believers themselves.

To facilitate "decently and in order," I have implemented a prophetic protocol that helps facilitate prophecy in our corporate gatherings. I have learned that implementing this kind of protocol communicates the process and procedure to believers, thereby removing the fear that comes with not knowing how to release a prophetic word in the corporate gathering. Here are the specifics of the prophetic protocol I have put in place:

1. Flow with the order of service. During the corporate gathering, there is a time during the worship that is conducive to prophecy. Often, there is a lull between choruses, where a prophetic word can be released. Prophetic people should watch the flow of the anointing created during this time. When the lull occurs, this is an ideal time to prophesy.

2. Prophesy from the front of the room. When I was a young believer, I observed people who were seated in the middle or back sections of the church who would stand and speak a prophecy from their seat. Prophecy, like the sermon, announcements and worship, should be given from the front of the church.

3. Use the microphone. Prophecy that cannot be heard by those who are present is unfruitful. Speak into the microphone so you can be heard. But avoid screaming. That is unfruitful, too.

4. Don't prophesy for too long. This is especially true when giving personal prophecy to someone. When you speak too long, people often tend to become tired or disengage. Deliver the message God has given you. Keep it accurate, and don't go too long.

5. Avoid repetition. When you prophesy, God has a specific message that He wants to convey. It might be one word. Repeating the same message over and over does not increase the accuracy. Don't overspiritualize the message through repetition. Say what you heard from God, then stop.

6. If you can't sing, don't. One of the ways to deliver a prophetic word is through song. In my ministry, worship is led by a prophet. Prophets who lead worship have a grace to hear and sing new songs. If you are

prophesying in a corporate gathering during worship, stay in the flow of the service. If the worship team is already singing the prophetic song you are hearing, don't go forward and sing the same song. If you are not a skillful singer, don't sing. The receiver will have difficulty receiving the message because of your lack of skill and grace in this area. Delivering the message in a conversational tone is just as powerful.

7. Have a teachable spirit. "Let two or three prophets speak, and let the others judge," 1 Corinthians 14:29 states. Prophecy is to be judged. Pastors and leaders in the ministry are responsible for the oversight of the ministry and therefore are responsible to judge prophetic words. Remain teachable. Resist pride. When you are given correction and instruction, be submissive.

8. Avoid strange demonstrations. Ezekiel was commanded to lie on his side for a certain number of days to prophetically demonstrate God's pending judgment against Israel (see Ezekiel 4). These types of prophetic demonstrations were common in Ezekiel's day but don't necessarily fit into today's culture. You don't want to appear spooky. You want the receiver to hear what the Lord is speaking and not become distracted by unusual behavior.

9. Know the prophetic protocol when you are visiting a church. It is inadvisable to prophesy if you do not know their protocol. In this case, wait until after the service and speak to one of the church leaders about the prophetic message you heard. Some church leaders might ask you to submit the word in writing. Don't be offended. Follow their protocol.

Reflection

How is the prophetic dimension operating in your life? Are you developing prophetic accuracy? Are you a member of a prophetic company? In other words, are you connected to mature prophets who can help you grow in the prophetic? If you are isolated, ask the Lord to lead you to a healthy prophetic community.

Prayer Activation

Lord Jesus, I thank You that You have anointed and called me to be a reformer. I will not be silent. Rather, I will allow the prophetic spirit within me to be ignited until it burns like fire. I confess that I am a believer, and I am anointed to prophesy.

6

The Force of the Anointing

The Spirit of the Lord is upon Me, because He has anointed
Me to preach the gospel to the poor; He has sent Me to heal
the broken-hearted, to preach deliverance to the captives, and
recovery of sight to the blind, to set at liberty those who are
oppressed; to preach the acceptable year of the Lord.

Luke 4:18–19

The anointing is God's supernatural force (ability) that
comes upon an individual, enabling him or her to function in the capacity God has predetermined. The terms *anoint*,
anointing or *anointed* appear more than one hundred fifty times
in the Bible. The frequency of these words indicates a measure
of significance. The *Dictionary of Bible Imagery* gives this definition: "Anointing usually means two things: it sets a person or
thing apart as holy and consecrated, and it confers authority
on a person who is anointed."[1] Priests, kings and prophets were
anointed, signifying their separation for God's holy purposes.

Jesus declared that He was anointed and sent. In chapters 4 and 5, we discussed the fact that apostles and prophets are "sent ones." Those who are aligned with apostles and prophets function as apostolic and prophetic believers. This happens as a result of having access to an impartation of the grace the apostles and prophets carry.

One Sabbath day in the synagogue at Nazareth, Jesus read this passage aloud from Isaiah 61:1–2, knowing that those present would be familiar with the Old Testament Scriptures:

> The Spirit of the Lord GOD is upon me because the LORD has anointed me to preach good news to the poor; He has sent me to heal the broken-hearted, to proclaim liberty to the captives, and the opening of the prison to those who are bound; to proclaim the acceptable year of the LORD.

In essence, Jesus declared several things about Himself when He quoted this passage:

- I am full of the Spirit.
- I am anointed to preach the Gospel to the poor.
- I am sent to heal the brokenhearted.
- I am sent to preach deliverance to the captives.
- I am sent to open blind eyes.
- I am sent to set at liberty those who are bruised.
- I am sent to preach the acceptable year of the Lord.

Looking at Jesus' declaration of these seven things about Himself, we can understand the purpose for which He was anointed. Purpose and anointing are linked. The anointing is the supernatural force of God operating within us to accomplish His purpose. To be anointed is to be smeared with purpose in the same way that Old Testament kings, priests and prophets were anointed with oil. You and I have been separated from the corruption of the world unto God's Kingdom purposes.

Application

Consider the list of descriptors Jesus gave in Luke 4:18–19, when He quoted the prophet Isaiah. Which of these characteristics are you strongest in? Which need more development in you?

The Increase of the Anointing

Dear one, the anointing is more than a catchy religious phrase. The anointing is power! To be anointed means that you are operating in the supernatural realm. "In that day the Lord will remove the heavy burden from your shoulders and break off the yoke of bondage from your necks because of the heavy anointing upon you!" (Isaiah 10:27 TPT). When you operate in the supernatural realm, God's ability is released through you. The anointing is about capacity—God's capacity operating in you to accomplish what He has purposed for your life.

God promised to break the yoke of bondage off His people's necks. Oxen were yoked for plowing the fields. To be yoked implies servitude, bondage or subjection. Yet by joining two animals together, yoking also is symbolic of a close alliance or union. This can be positive or negative. Oxen and donkeys are both beasts of burden, but to yoke them together was forbidden in the Old Testament (see Deuteronomy 22:10). When discussing marriage, Paul uses the idea of being yoked when he commands believers to refrain from marrying unbelievers: "Do not be unequally yoked together with unbelievers" (2 Corinthians 6:14). Jesus, however, invites us to take His yoke upon us so that we can be in close union with Him and learn His ways: "Take My yoke upon you, and learn from Me. For I am meek and lowly in heart, and you will find rest for your souls. For My yoke is easy, and My burden is light" (Matthew 11:29–30).

Anointing is connected to fatness. This type of fatness is related to blessing and increase. Another way to understand fatness is capacity. As well-fed oxen increase in size, the yoke becomes too small for them. In other words, the capacity of the oxen increases. This is also a picture of enlargement. The more you increase your spiritual capacity through prayer, study of the Word and worship, the more any yokes of bondage the enemy attempts to place upon you will break. Your spiritual capacity includes operating in faith. When you operate in faith, the enemy cannot place a yoke of doubt and unbelief upon you. Faith is a characteristic of believers. Faith empowers us to operate as Kingdom influencers.

Anointing and Identity

As I mentioned, Jesus declared that the Spirit was upon Him and that He was anointed. Throughout His ministry, He continued to declare what He was anointed to do. Jesus was established in His identity and purpose. He knew "who" He was and "what" He was anointed and sent to do. Let's look at the Luke 4:18–19 passage in a different version, The Passion Translation:

> The Spirit of the Lord is upon me, and he has anointed me to be hope for the poor, healing for the brokenhearted, and new eyes for the blind, and to preach to prisoners, "You are set free!" I have come to share the message of Jubilee, for the time of God's great acceptance has begun.

Anointing is linked with identity. Many believers have not fully understood their identity and purpose. They don't know the purpose of God for their lives. In other words, they don't know why God created them. Dear one, when you don't know why

God created you, the anointing cannot fully flow. Ignorance in this area restricts the anointing. Jesus has given us the anointing to labor with Him in building the Church. He declared that He would build His Church. He is using the gifts of apostles and prophets on earth to co-labor with Him by equipping the believers to do the work of the ministry. As sent ones, apostles and prophets activate believers in the area of the anointing, gift and call God has assigned them. As accurate Kingdom builders, apostles and prophets are anointed to lay the foundation of truth, as Ephesians 2:20 (TPT) shows:

> You are rising like the perfectly fitted stones of the temple; and your lives have been built up together upon the foundation laid by the apostles and prophets, and best of all, you are connected to the Head Cornerstone of the building, the Anointed One, Jesus Christ himself!

This Scripture indicates that the Church is built on the foundation laid by the apostles and prophets. This means that the apostles and prophets set the tone and agenda for the Church, activating its people to function as Kingdom believers who have been anointed to carry out the mandate of heaven and overcome the darkness. The foundation the apostles and prophets laid establishes believers in truth, forming them into a spiritual house that the powers of darkness cannot shake.

Without the anointing, the Church becomes stagnant. Consider natural water sources. Water currents create movement, whereas standing water such as a pond can become stagnant. Stagnant water fosters bacteria. When the Church becomes stagnant, it becomes legalistic and develops a rules-based culture. The anointing, however, releases a supernatural current within us, moving and stirring us to advance.

Each believer has been given a measure of grace to participate in the building process (see Romans 12:3; Ephesians 4:7).

You have been given a measure of grace. *Strong's Concordance* key #3358 tells us that the word *measure* is taken from the word *metron*, which means "a portion or allotment." We can see this in Genesis where God placed Adam and Eve in the Garden and assigned them a portion (*metron*) to oversee. You have been given a measure that is connected to the purpose God has planned for you. The anointing is God's supernatural force operating in you to accomplish His plans. The anointing that God has given you empowers you to influence those around you through evangelism, preaching, healing the sick and delivering those who are spiritually bound. The anointing opens the eyes of the lost, enabling them to "see" the glorious truth of God's love for them. You must commit to walking in the anointing daily. You must also commit to enlarging your spiritual capacity.

Increasing the Anointing

As you grow and develop, the anointing increases. When I consider the anointing on my life, I can see how it has continued to increase. During my travels in ministry, it is not uncommon for people to ask me how they can receive the anointing and how they can grow in it. My response is always centered around the eight keys listed below, which I offer for your consideration.

1. *Prayer*. A consistent life of prayer is the foundation for increasing the anointing in your life.
2. *Study of the Word of God*. Knowing God's Word is one way of knowing Him. Knowing His Word fills you with desire to experience Him more deeply.
3. *Worship*. Worship brings you into God's presence, where you encounter Him in significant ways.

4. *Faith.* You must have faith to believe that God wants you to operate in greater and greater measures of the anointing.

5. *Obedience.* You must purpose to be led by the Spirit of God. Whatever He tells you, do it quickly.

6. *Impartation.* Being around people who are anointed, reading books and attending conferences focused on Jesus and His will are keys to increasing the anointing.

7. *Walking in the anointing.* The anointing has a purpose. As you walk in the anointing, it will increase.

8. *Sacrifice.* The anointing is costly and will cost you everything. Beyond obedience lies sacrifice. This is the place where we surrender time, entertainment and other such things, that we might walk deeply in the anointing. These things are not always sacrificed forever, but expect times when the Lord will call you to "come away" with Him for a while. This does not mean you resign from your job, leave your family or do some other outlandish thing. It means that sometimes you will need to pull aside to be with the Lord.

Shallow Living

Too many believers are content with living shallow, ineffective lives. Carnality among believers has become commonplace. Teaching on the dangers of carnality and fleshly living has been replaced by self-help empowerment messages that lack the power and authority Jesus has given the Church. I consider this spiritual malnourishment.

Smoke machines have taken the place of the smoke of the Lord's presence rising as believers abandon themselves to Him in corporate worship. Light shows during worship have taken the place of the Shekinah glory of the Lord. Stages have taken the place of the altar. Don't miss my point here. From an aesthetic perspective, I am in favor of preparing the sanctuary in ways that make the space warm and inviting. Yet when the "church show" takes the place of God's presence, I see this as problematic.

Believers have resigned themselves to the place of spectating rather than participating. Celebrations of joy, clapping our hands, rejoicing, bowing, singing, spinning and dancing in God's presence have been replaced by shallowness. We have forgotten what it means to "burn with passionate desire" for the One who loves us unconditionally.

Activation

Review the list of keys I have found that increase the anointing. What areas has the Lord been speaking to you about? Don't rush this process. Be prepared to spend time with the Lord and allow Him to speak to you.

The Anointing Is Supernatural

The anointing shifts us into the supernatural realm, beyond what is possible in our human ability. When you operate in the realm of the supernatural, your capacity to influence those around you increases exponentially.

The apostle Paul manifested Kingdom anointing during his appeal before King Agrippa. As Paul finished speaking, King Agrippa said, "You almost persuade me to become a Christian" (Acts 26:28). This is a picture of the force of the anointing. When you speak or minister under the anointing, your anointed words and actions manifest God's force.

Make no mistake about this fact: *You are anointed.* The supernatural force of God is ready to operate through you to bring the kingdom of darkness down and exalt the Kingdom of

God. Our next chapter will focus on the supernatural weapons God has given you to accomplish this.

Reflection

We discussed the fact that the anointing gives you supernatural power to do what you could not otherwise do. How do you see the anointing operating in your life? When is your anointing strongest? When is it weakest? Submit your weak areas to the Lord. Thank Him for the areas where you are strong.

Prayer Activation

I decree that Jesus will rise and shine in my life, heart, ministry, family, city, region and nation as "the Bright and Morning Star" (Revelation 22:16). Lord, I ask You to arise in greater measure and degree. I open my heart and say, "Arise, O Lord, in me!"[2]

PART 3

Armed and Dangerous

This third and final section of the book will focus on our weaponry. You and I have been given supernatural weapons. Another way to understand this is to know that God has given us a supernatural arsenal. As we commit to worship and war, we will win. Worshiping warriors receive heaven's supernatural strategies that increase their capacity to win over the powers of darkness. When we win, we gather the spoils of the enemy, which are the souls locked in darkness. We are armed and dangerous!

7

Supernatural Weapons

For although we live in the natural realm, we don't wage a military campaign employing human weapons, using manipulation to achieve our aims. Instead, our spiritual weapons are energized with divine power to effectively dismantle the defenses behind which people hide. We can demolish every deceptive fantasy that opposes God and break through every arrogant attitude that is raised up in defiance of the true knowledge of God. We capture, like prisoners of war, every thought and insist that it bow in obedience to the Anointed One.

2 Corinthians 10:3–5 TPT

Inaccurate teaching has influenced the Church to believe that spiritual warfare is no longer necessary. Many believers passively wait for their life or the world to end so that they can go to heaven and receive their crown. They are not engaged in advancing their Kingdom mandate. They are simply celebrating their salvation, and rightly so. The problem with this way of thinking is that too often it lacks any focus on using our influence as we walk in Kingdom power and authority. I call this "living in the waiting room," which happens when you succumb to a spirit of passivity. Instead, you must remain vigilant and alert.

From generation to generation, all believers are called to war against the powers of darkness until the demonic grip on humanity is broken. Dear one, this includes you. You cannot fulfill your Kingdom assignment without warfare. You must commit daily to standing against the kingdom of darkness and battling Satan's forces wherever they present themselves in your garden. Remember, like Adam and Eve, we have each been assigned a garden or portion to tend. To ensure your victory, God has given you supernatural weapons. These weapons are not adornments. They are powerful, demon-busting weapons that operate by faith and are vital to securing your victory.

In the apostle Paul's statement we just read from 2 Corinthians 10:3–4 (TPT), "Our spiritual weapons are energized with divine power to effectively dismantle the defenses behind which people hide," he reminded the early believers of the power of the weapons God had given them. Today, his statement also reminds you and me that our warfare is not a natural war fought with natural weapons. Our human intellect is insufficient to overcome darkness. Our powerful weapons are supernatural—meaning they are not natural in origin, but make up a supernatural arsenal that is fully capable of defeating darkness.

It is important to understand how to use your spiritual weaponry and to know the rules of engagement that govern your warfare. This is an area where too many believers lack understanding. It is an area of weakness wherein the enemy can gain an advantage. Remember, we talked earlier about how ignorance simply means to have a lack of knowledge or information. In 2 Corinthians 2:11, the apostle Paul encouraged the Corinthian Church, and also us, not to be ignorant of the enemy's tactics. Do not lack understanding. Understanding the rules of engagement and knowing your weaponry is vital to your success in spiritual warfare.

Rules of Engagement

The *Encyclopedia Britannica* defines "rules of engagement" this way:

> Formally, rules of engagement refer to the orders issued by a competent military authority that delineate when, where, how, and against whom military forces may be used, and they have implications for what actions soldiers may take on their own authority and what directions may be issued by a commanding officer.[1]

In similar manner to theaters of war on natural battlefields, your spiritual warfare is subject to spiritual rules of engagement. Let's examine Ephesians 6:10–18 here and in the next section, which covers your battle gear. This will lead us to discover our spiritual rules of engagement and the supernatural weapons God has given us. (All Scriptures in the following list are from The Passion Translation.)

Rule of Engagement #1: *Be strong.*
"Be supernaturally infused with strength through your life-union with the Lord Jesus" (Ephesians 6:10).

Rule of Engagement #2: *Keep standing.*
"Stand victorious with the force of his explosive power flowing in and through you" (Ephesians 6:10).

Rule of Engagement #3: *Get dressed.*
"Put on God's complete set of armor provided for us, so that you will be protected as you fight against the evil strategies of the accuser!" (Ephesians 6:11).

Rule of Engagement #4: *Know your enemy.*
"Your hand-to-hand combat is not with human beings, but with the highest principalities and authorities operating in rebellion under the heavenly realms"
(Ephesians 6:12).

Rule of Engagement #5: *Don't underestimate your enemy.*
"For they are a powerful class of demon-gods and
evil spirits that hold this dark world in bondage" (Ephesians 6:12).

Rule of Engagement #6: *Remember you are protected.*
"Because of this, you must wear all the armor that
God provides so you're protected as you confront the
slanderer" (Ephesians 6:13).

Rule of Engagement#7: *You are destined to win.*
"Pray passionately in the Spirit, as you constantly
intercede with every form of prayer at all times" (Ephesians 6:18).

Following these rules of engagement positions you to win. Regardless of the intensity and duration of your battle, you will
be victorious.

Your Battle Gear

Scripture commands us to put on the whole armor of God. It
is an error to think that God will put the armor on you. God
provides the battle gear, but you must be intentional about
wearing your supernatural armor daily. The armor is not designed à la carte, where you can choose the portions you will
wear. We are commanded to put on the "whole" armor. Whole
speaks of entirety.

As believers, we must take onto ourselves the whole armor. Your spiritual armor is divided into defensive and offensive armor:

- *Defensive armor:* This protects us and includes the helmet of salvation, the girdle or belt of truth, the breastplate of righteousness, Gospel shoes and the shield of faith.
- *Offensive armor:* This injures the attacker and is the sword of the Spirit.

When you receive Christ, you receive your spiritual armor designed to protect you from the onslaughts of the enemy. Remember that your battle is not a natural battle. It is supernatural and must be fought with spiritual weapons. Your weapons have their origination in God's strength, and when you operate in faith, your weapons "effectively dismantle the defenses behind which people hide" (2 Corinthians 10:4 TPT). This is a picture of how your influence is infused with the power of God, resulting in a tremendous harvest of souls into the Kingdom.

In 2 Corinthians 10:5–6 (TPT), we see some of the things we can accomplish when we use our supernatural weapons:

We can demolish every deceptive fantasy that opposes God and break through every arrogant attitude that is raised up in defiance of the true knowledge of God. We capture, like prisoners of war, every thought and insist that it bow in obedience to the Anointed One. Since we are armed with such dynamic weaponry, we stand ready to punish any trace of rebellion, as soon as you choose complete obedience."

You are anointed to prevail over the kingdom of darkness. Arguments and the vain philosophies of mankind are refuted as you engage and overcome the enemy. Let's take a few minutes to review our battle gear.

135

Belt of Truth

"Put on truth as a belt to strengthen you to stand in triumph" (Ephesians 6:14 TPT). The first piece of armor we buckle on is the girdle or belt of truth. In the natural world, a suit of armor was attached to the belt, which held the other pieces of armor in place. The truth of God's Word is the spiritual belt to which all the other pieces of our armor are attached. As Satan did with Eve in the Garden, he will make every attempt to attack the truth through deception and distortion. But the truth will protect you from lies, deception, distortion and doctrinal errors of the enemy. The belt of truth helps you stand in triumph and holds your other pieces of armor in place. In the natural, human reproductive organs are housed in your loins. In the spiritual, when you put on the belt of truth, whatever you produce is anchored in truth.

Breastplate of Righteousness

"Put on holiness as the protective armor that covers your heart" (Ephesians 6:14 TPT). Visually, the breastplate was similar to an ancient corselet, which covered the upper body. In the natural, the breastplate protected the vital organs (heart, lungs, etc.). You do not stand justified before God based on your own righteousness or merits. You have been given the spiritual breastplate of righteousness, which refers to the righteousness of Christ. This is our spiritual protection that protects our spiritual vital organs from the attacks of Satan and from unrighteousness (see 2 Corinthians 6:7; Philippians 3:9). Christ has fought and won your battles through His righteousness. He has triumphed over darkness, and now you must receive the righteousness of God by faith and enforce those victories as you advance the Kingdom of God (see Colossians 2:15). The breastplate of righteousness is secured in place by the belt of truth. Righteousness and truth are important weapons.

Gospel Shoes

"Stand on your feet alert, then you'll always be ready to share the blessings of peace" (Ephesians 6:15 TPT). Having appropriate protection for your feet is vital to your effectiveness as a warrior. God has provided you with shoes designed for warfare. Spiritual shoes are connected to your spiritual walk. How you walk is the same as how you live before the Lord and before unbelievers. Shoes help you advance over rugged terrain. In the same manner, wearing the preparation of the Gospel of peace as your footwear protects you from temptation. The enemy will attempt to lead you down wrong paths, but having your feet shod with the preparation of the Gospel of peace will protect you (see Romans 13:12–14). Reception of the Gospel brings peace between God and man. As a Kingdom influencer, you must be willing to do every good work to spread the Gospel to all people, nations, tribes and tongues. This must be your daily commitment.

Shield of Faith

"In every battle, take faith as your wrap-around shield, for it is able to extinguish the blazing arrows coming at you from the evil one!" (Ephesians 6:16 TPT). The shield referenced here refers to a shield that covered the entire body. Believers are made righteous through faith in the shed blood of Christ. We are not righteous through self-effort, only through the blood of Jesus. This revelatory truth is a weapon against the enemy. The fiery darts of the enemy are unable to pierce the shield of faith. These darts or arrows attempt to attack your mind with doubt and unbelief about your identity in Christ. As your mind is renewed in the Word, however, your shield is renewed.

Helmet of Salvation

"Embrace the power of salvation's full deliverance, like a helmet to protect your thoughts from lies" (Ephesians 6:17–18 TPT).

The helmets that Roman soldiers wore were engraved with various emblematic figures that represented their hope. The believer's hope is in Christ (see 1 Thessalonians 5:8). As *Clarke's Commentary* puts it, "So the hope of conquering every adversary and surmounting every difficulty, through the blood of the Lamb, is a helmet that protects the head."[2] The helmet of salvation represents a regenerated mind and also a transformed and renewed thought life. The helmet of salvation protects your mind from Satan's lies and deceptions. He desperately fights for control of the mind. An undisciplined mind makes you easy prey to the sinful deceptions of the enemy. The primary battlefield of the enemy is against your mind. Renewing your mind daily strengthens you in that area (see Romans 12:1–2; Philippians 4:7).

Sword of the Spirit

"And take the mighty razor-sharp Spirit-sword of the spoken word of God" (Ephesians 6:17–18 TPT). The "sword of the Spirit" is the Word of God. It is both a defensive and offensive weapon. Jesus spent forty days and nights in the wilderness, after which Satan confronted Him (see Matthew 4:1–11). In each of the three temptations Satan presented, Jesus used the Word of God. As a believer, your defense against the tactics and temptations of the enemy is the Word of God. Sharper than a two-edged sword, the Word of God is effective in defending you against the lies and deceitful tactics of the enemy (see Hebrews 4:12). Regular study of God's Word will prepare you to face off the enemy whenever and wherever he presents himself in your life.

Support Weapons

As a believer, you have been given a powerful arsenal of supernatural weapons to overcome the forces of darkness. You are armed and dangerous. To facilitate the use of your weapons, here are some other attributes of next-level believers that I believe will help keep you moving forward as you push back the darkness.

Prayer

"Pray passionately in the Spirit, as you constantly intercede with every form of prayer at all times. Pray the blessings of God upon all his believers" (Ephesians 6:18 TPT). Prayer is a discipline many believers often neglect. A consistent prayer life helps keep you in tune with the Spirit of God. When you pray in the name of Jesus, you are using your delegated power and authority.

Tongues

"They were all filled and equipped with the Holy Spirit and were inspired to speak in tongues—empowered by the Spirit to speak in languages they had never learned!" (Acts 2:4 TPT). God has armed you as a believer with a supernatural language. This is praying in the Spirit. When you pray in the Spirit, it strengthens you and you receive revelation (see Zechariah 4:6; Acts 1:8; 1 Corinthians 14:4; Jude 20–21). Praying in tongues, or praying in the Spirit, edifies you and activates the gifts of the Spirit within you.

Binding and Loosing

"I will give you the keys of heaven's kingdom realm to forbid on earth that which is forbidden in heaven, and to release on earth that which is released in heaven" (Matthew 16:19 TPT). God has given you the keys of the Kingdom and has deployed you as a militant reformer. This is a manifestation of the keys of power and authority He has also given you. Understanding the principle of binding and loosing is an important strategy in overcoming the power of the enemy.

In other words, you need to know what to bind and what to loose. Gaining revelation and understanding about God's will can help you understand the weapon of binding and loosing. God has fully authorized you to forbid and/or release things on earth, with heaven's support backing up your actions. Matthew 18:18 (TPT) tells us, "Receive this truth: Whatever you forbid on earth will be considered to be forbidden in heaven, and whatever you release on earth will be considered to be released in heaven."

Prayers, decrees and confessions based on God's Word are the ways that we bind and loose. You are fully authorized to bind the power of the enemy in your life, home, community and ministry. You are equipped to loose men and women from the bondage of sin, depression and discouragement from the enemy. You have been fully authorized to walk in this kind of power and authority. Earlier in this book, we talked about our voice and the power of our words. Use your voice to release God's will. When you do this, the enemy will be defeated.

The Name and Blood of Jesus

One of the Scriptures most frequently used to describe the believer's authority is found in Mark 16:17–18 (TPT):

> These miracle signs will accompany those who believe: They will drive out demons in the power of my name. They will speak in tongues. They will be supernaturally protected from snakes and from drinking anything poisonous. And they will lay hands on the sick and heal them.

I have heard this passage quoted and taught numerous times. I use it when explaining the Kingdom job description of believers. Yet not until recently did I begin emphasizing "how" we are able to cast out devils, heal the sick, speak with new tongues and receive supernatural protection from evil. Our authority is in the name of Jesus. His name is higher than any named sickness or disease. Demons fear the name of Jesus because they know He defeated them at Calvary (see Matthew 28:18–20; Ephesians 1:21).

Along with the name of Jesus, the power of the blood of Jesus is a weapon. By faith in the blood of Jesus, you received salvation. Satan was not defeated by mere words. The obedience of Jesus was unto death on the cross (see Philippians 2:8), and on the third day He was resurrected by the Father. Jesus defeated death and the enemy's principalities and powers, and so restored dominion over all things to humankind. Satan was conquered!

Although Jesus conquered Satan at Calvary, the enemy is still at large, and his forces of demonic powers, the flesh and the world are still at war in the land. They attempt to control territory that is rightfully that of the Conqueror, Jesus. They work to blind humanity to the good news of the Gospel (see 2 Corinthians 4:3; Colossians 1:26–29). Satan wants to blind people to the truth of his defeat and the fact that he is under judgment. He and his forces try to control homes, churches and nations. You and I have been dispatched, however, to carry the Kingdom message. We must open the eyes of men and women to the enemy's deception and regain control of territory that is rightfully ours. This is a lifelong assignment, one which we execute in the name of Jesus.

Praise and Worship

Our praise is a weapon against the enemy. Amos 9:11 (AMP) states, "In that day I shall raise up and restore the fallen tabernacle (booth) of David. And wall up its breaches [in the city walls]; I will also raise up and restore its ruins and rebuild it as it was in the days of old." God promised to restore the tabernacle of David, which hosted His presence twenty-four hours a day, seven days a week. David hired singers and musicians to offer continual praise and worship to God.

Although Moses had built a tabernacle, it was David's tabernacle God promised to restore. Amos 9:12 (AMP), tells us why: "That they may possess the remnant of Edom (ancient enemies) and all the nations that are called by My name." Unlike the tabernacle of Moses, David's tabernacle did not have a veil of separation between the priests and the presence of the Lord. This absence of a veil pointed to a time when there would be no separation between God and His people. David was a reformer who wrote psalms, which are prophetic songs, and he praised God without fear of what others would think (see 2 Samuel 6:16–20).

God is restoring David's tabernacle so that we might possess the land. Praise and worship are weapons against the enemy. When you praise and worship God, you punish principalities and powers in the Spirit (see Psalm 149:5–9). Praise and worship are connected to sound. Remember that everything in the earth realm is voice activated. Praise and worship involve the skillful execution of words and movement, which honors God and defeats your enemies. Whether you have a melodic voice or not, you must become comfortable using the weapons of praise and worship.

Application

Praise and worship are not passive. Consider how you worship and give praise to God. Are you comfortable expressing praise? Take several days to consider any reasons or areas where you feel discomfort in your praise. Submit those areas to the Lord and begin taking time in your home to express praise. Finally, let the faith arise in you to express praise and worship in corporate gatherings.

Spiritual Boot Camps

As I said at the beginning of this chapter, the supernatural weaponry God has given us involves more than adornments. You and I have been armed to war and win against the kingdom of Satan. Yet we can also train to increase our effectiveness.

In a natural army, soldiers endure significant weapons training. They are also subjected to rigorous physical training designed to build stamina and increase their capacity. This training is called boot camp. As a believer, it is important that you spend time in spiritual boot camps designed to bring you into a balanced understanding of how to use your weapons. For example, often you can find conferences, webinars and Schools of the Prophets events that offer more intensive training and activation for next-level believers. Such boot camps will build your stamina and increase your spiritual capacity. This is how you will become effective in your warfare against darkness.

Your battle against darkness is daily and will last the entire span of your life. You are equipped to win, so don't settle for failure!

Reflection

Review the battle gear I outlined in this chapter. Spend time each day reading Scriptures on each of the weapons I presented. Commit these Scriptures to memory for easy recall when you need them.

Prayer Activation

Lord, thank You for the spiritual armor You have provided for me. I confess that I am a heavily armed soldier. I decree that I will stand strong in the power of the Spirit, using my weapons to defeat the powers of darkness. I decree that I will not leave my assigned position. Rather, I will stand strong, in Jesus' name.

8

The Weapon of Faith

Now faith is the assurance (title deed, confirmation) of things
hoped for (divinely guaranteed), and the evidence of things not
seen [the conviction of their reality—faith comprehends as fact
what cannot be experienced by the physical senses].

Hebrews 11:1 AMP

Faith is mentioned in the Scriptures more than three hundred
times. This level of frequency tells us that God wants us not
only to understand faith, but also to cultivate faith that will
enable us to carry out the mission He has given us. Faith is the
substance we stand on. *Strong's Concordance* key #5287 defines *substance* as "a setting or placing under . . . substructure,
foundation." The substance of faith is steadfastness of mind,
firmness, courage, resolution, confidence, firm trust or assurance. Faith is also the evidence of what has not yet manifested.
We stand on the foundation of resolute confidence, knowing
that what we hope for will manifest. Faith is not wishing or

belief-ism. Faith is steadfastness of mind and courage whereon you position yourself expectantly, waiting for God's promise to manifest.

There are two types of faith—natural and spiritual. Natural faith is something everyone possesses. Farmers have faith that their crops will grow because they sowed seed. Employees perform their jobs in advance of payment, believing that they will be paid on the designated day. These are examples of natural faith. Natural faith is different than spiritual faith. Spiritual faith is the key by which we operate in the spiritual realm. We receive salvation by faith. We are justified by faith, not on our own merit. We do not have access to God based on our own merit. We have access through faith in the blood of Jesus. By faith, we understand that the universe was framed by the word of God, so that things that are seen were not made out of things that are visible (see Hebrews 11:3). By faith, we believe that God's Word is true and that He is incapable of lying.

Faith pleases God. "But without faith it is impossible to [walk with God and] please Him, for whoever comes [near] to God must [necessarily] believe that God exists and that He rewards those who [earnestly and diligently] seek Him" (Hebrews 11:6 AMP). God rewards our confidence that He will perform His Word by performing His Word. Faith does not waver, but fully expects its object to manifest. As James 1:6 says of anyone asking God for wisdom, "But let him ask in faith, without wavering. For he who wavers is like a wave of the sea, driven and tossed with the wind."

Faith is supernatural in its core as it sees what has not happened as though it has already happened. As a firm foundation on which you stand, faith is not moved by time or circumstance. Faith is believing God, trusting and knowing that He will manifest His Word. I have often stated that faith is like a hand, reaching into the unseen and bringing forth God's promises into the earthly realm.

What Faith Is

Faith is productive. We begin with a prophetic promise of God. As we continue to stand on the fact that what God has promised, He will perform, what started as a mustard seed now becomes fully developed (see Mark 4:31; Luke 17:6). Faith based on God's Word produces continuously as we go from faith to faith (see Luke 17:5).

In other words, you grow in faith. Your race as a believer began in faith, as you repented of your sins and accepted the finished work of Christ at Calvary. That is saving faith. As you grow and develop in spiritual things, your faith grows. I am not referencing size here. I am referring to the object of your faith—that which you are believing God for. Just as you trusted confidently and believed that God had received you into His family when you prayed and surrendered your life, now you have faith that when you exercise the authority and power He has given you, He responds.

Faith is the supernatural capacity of God working in you to believe. Our human faith is limited. Faith sees God's promises as done. Faith knows that God watches over His Word to perform what He has said.

> As the snow and rain that fall from heaven do not return until they have accomplished their purpose, soaking the earth and causing it to sprout with new life, providing seed to sow and bread to eat. So also will be the word that I speak; it does not return to me unfulfilled. My word performs my purpose *and fulfills the mission I sent it out to accomplish.*
>
> Isaiah 55:10–11 TPT, emphasis added

Faith doesn't "guess" that God will do what He has said. Faith accepts as fact that God will do what He has said. Faith fully expects God to perform His Word.

Faith is now! Hebrews 11:1 says, "Now faith is . . ." Faith is the present. *Now.* It is the foundation of what you are hoping for. This is not the "cross your fingers" and hope position. People's hope is often filled with unbelief. Unbelief is the antithesis of faith. You and I are not passively waiting and partially expecting that what God has said won't manifest. No, we are radically standing on the Word of God, expecting nothing less than manifestation.

John 11:38–44 gives us the account of Lazarus being miraculously raised from the dead. When Jesus called him by name, there was no doubt in Jesus' mind that Lazarus would be restored to life and would emerge from the tomb, the place of death. Jesus was operating in "now faith" when He called Lazarus back to life.

Faith Is a Key

You have unlimited access to the gifts of the Spirit, revelation and every supernatural support you need from heaven. The key to successful engagement is faith. Let's look at three key types of faith: the gift of faith, the weapon of faith and the fruit of faith.

The Gift of Faith

The gift of faith is different from faith as a fruit of the Spirit. The gift of faith is supernatural capacity to believe God for impossible things. Elijah operated in supernatural faith when he informed King Ahab that it would not rain for three years, until the prophet himself called forth rain (see 1 Kings 17:1). Elisha operated in supernatural faith when he raised the widow's son from the dead (see 2 Kings 4:8–37).

When Jesus called Lazarus from the tomb, He was operating in the gift of faith. Peter operated in the gift of faith when he healed a man who had been lame since birth (see Acts 3). He also operated in the gift of faith when he pronounced judgment on Ananias and Sapphira, who attempted to deceive the church (see Acts 5). Peter pronounced judgment that resulted in their immediate death.

While those who operate in the power gifts of healings and miracles operate in the gift of faith, there are also other types of miracles performed through the gift of faith.

The Weapon of Faith

The Bible mentions several types of faith, for example, saving faith, the gift of faith and the spiritual fruit of faith. Ephesians 6:16 commands us to take up the shield of faith. In this context, faith is a weapon used to quench the fiery darts of the enemy. Those fiery darts are unbelief, fear and rejection. They are like missiles the enemy launches against you. This is why you must be renewed in the spirit of your mind (see Ephesians 4:23). The enemy wants you to believe that you are not anointed like other believers. Yet the fact is that God has given you a measure of faith (see Romans 12:3). This measure creates the supernatural foundation that you stand on as you confidently trust God for salvation, deliverance, healing and operating in the gifts of the Spirit.

God has called and anointed you to flow in the gifts of the Spirit. He has given a measure of grace to every believer, and that includes you. The word *faith*, when used in relation to the shield of faith, speaks of defensive faith. This faith is unwavering trust and resolute confidence in God, who protects you from the flaming missiles of doubt and unbelief the enemy sends your way. Your shield of faith does not include anxiety, but rather confidence. Your confidence is not based on your abilities, but on the power of God. Faith as a shield therefore deflects the fiery darts and arrows of the enemy.

You are called to war against the enemy. Each weapon God has given you empowers you to be victorious as you overcome evil.

Overcome every form of evil as a victorious soldier of Jesus the Anointed One. For every soldier called to active duty must divorce himself from the distractions of this world so that he may fully satisfy the one who chose him.

An athlete who doesn't play by the rules will never receive the trophy, so remain faithful to God!

2 Timothy 2:3–5 TPT

The Fruit of Faith

Faith is a fruit of the Spirit. "But the fruit of the Spirit is love, joy, peace, patience, gentleness, goodness, faith, meekness, and self-control; against such there is no law" (Galatians 5:22–23). The command to be fruitful first appears in Genesis, where we read the account of Creation. The word *fruit* appears more than two hundred times in Scripture.[1] The first transgression in the Garden involved fruit. Eve took fruit from the tree of the knowledge of good and evil, and together, she and Adam ate it (see Genesis 3:6). Fruit can be good or evil (see Matthew 7:17–19; Luke 6:43). It also produces an outcome. The outcome produced in Adam and Eve was shame, pain and suffering, and ultimately death (see Genesis 3:7; 16–19).

God designed everything in the created order to reproduce and multiply. This is a picture of fruitfulness. It is also a picture of abundance and increase. In the Old Testament, godly people are described as trees (see Psalm 1:3; Jeremiah 17:8). In the New Testament, we see references to the fruit of repentance, and Jesus taught that trees could be identified by their fruit (see Matthew 3:8–10; 7:15–20). God created you with the capacity to produce fruit. Every decision you make produces fruit. The type of fruit you produce depends on the source of the seed. Using the term *works* to describe fruit, the apostle Paul distinguishes this fact in Galatians 5:16–21. As you yield to the work of the Spirit, the fruit produced in your life will reflect Christ.

God uses everything in our lives to produce the character of Jesus in us. This is the fruit of the Spirit. There is a difference between the fruit of the Spirit and the gifts of the Spirit. Gifts are given supernaturally to every believer. The key idea in this is that the gifts are *given*. The fruit of the Spirit, however, is *developed* over time. This speaks of process. In the same way as a natural seed is planted in the ground and develops into a mature state over time, the fruit of the Spirit is developed in us over the course of time. As believers, we are to develop the character of Jesus.

As you grow and mature in your walk with Christ, you will produce fruit. Jesus put it this way: "I am the vine, you are the branches. He who remains in Me, and I in him, bears much fruit. For without Me you can do nothing" (John 15:5). Plants in an earthly garden are watered and weeded. God does the same with you, as Jesus explained: "Every branch in Me that bears no fruit, He takes away. And every branch that bears fruit, He prunes, that it may bear more fruit" (John 15:2).

God carefully prunes each of us. He prunes away the dead or underdeveloped areas of our lives, which involves a cutting process. This can be painful, but it is necessary. As you submit your life to God's tender care, He is faithful to remove every dead area that is preventing you from developing the fruit of the Spirit. Not only does God want you to develop the fruit of the Spirit, but He also wants your life to produce much fruit.

Jesus and Faith

Jesus is the author and finisher of our faith (see Hebrews 12:2). Keeping your focus on Jesus and not allowing the distractions and entanglements of life to overtake you is vital to developing a strong "faith walk." Many concerns will clamor for your attention, but you must endeavor to keep your eyes fixed on Jesus. Keep your eyes on the goal (see 1 Corinthians 9:24–25; Philippians 3:14).

During His earthly ministry, Jesus demonstrated the power of faith. Every miracle He performed was the outworking of faith and dependency on His Father. In John 5:30 He said, "I can do nothing of Myself. As I hear, I judge. My judgment is just, because I seek not My own will, but the will of the Father who sent Me." Every miracle Jesus performed, He performed as a man. He is our example. Through His life, death, burial and resurrection, we have access to the Father, and we receive power. The power we receive is the same power Jesus walked in.

The disciples were with Jesus, watching Him heal the sick, cast out demons, raise the dead and feed five thousand men (this number does not include the women and children who were with them). Yet the disciples did not fully perceive the importance of faith (see Matthew 8:26; 14:31; 16:8). Sadly, many believers today do not understand faith and its operation either.

How Faith Operates

The Kingdom operates by faith. Without faith, you have no grasp of truth. Without faith you cannot receive salvation (see Hebrews 11:6). Without faith you cannot claim the righteousness of Christ and walk effectively in the authority and power God has given you.

As I stated earlier, faith is not belief-ism. It is not presumption, assumption, speculation or guessing. Faith is the foundation, based on God's Word, on which we stand. The more you seek God, the more your faith increases (see Romans 1:17; 10:17; Hebrews 12:2).

Acting on God's Word is another way to increase your faith. Faith gives us the supernatural capacity to overcome the world (see 1 John 5:4). Everything God has given to you—salvation, deliverance, gifts, supernatural weapons, etc.—are all activated by faith. It is time to make the same dynamic request the disciples made of Jesus: *Lord, increase my faith* (see Luke 17:5).

Reflection

Take time to read and meditate on the Scriptures mentioned in this chapter. Commit as many as possible to memory. Include them in your times of prayer, and decree them over your life. After several weeks, examine how your faith is increasing.

Prayer Activation

Lord, I agree with Hebrews 11:1. I decree that faith is my "assurance (title deed, confirmation) of things hoped for (divinely guaranteed), and the evidence of things not seen [the conviction of their reality—faith comprehends as fact what cannot be experienced by the physical senses]" [AMP]. I look to Jesus, the author and finisher of my faith, confidently knowing that I am His, I am victorious and I am fruitful.

9

Supernatural Capacity

But the manifestation of the Spirit is given to everyone for the common good. To one is given by the Spirit the word of wisdom, to another the word of knowledge by the same Spirit, to another faith by the same Spirit, to another gifts of healings by the same Spirit, to another the working of miracles, to another prophecy, to another discerning of spirits, to another various kinds of tongues, and to another the interpretation of tongues. But that one and very same Spirit works all these, dividing to each one individually as He will.

1 Corinthians 12:7–11

My desire in this chapter is to take you into a deeper understanding of the gifts of the Spirit and how these supernatural gifts are designed to help you expand your Kingdom influence. I want you to consider the gifts, which are activated by the Holy Spirit, as supernatural weapons that God has given you. When you operate in the gifts of the Spirit, your capacity to move in those gifts and thereby influence others supernaturally enlarges. The way I like to put it is, "When I will, He will. When He wills, I will." It is a matter of cooperating with the Holy Spirit. The gifts operating through you and me can influence unbelievers to surrender their lives to God, who is actively pursuing them. God's power is released through the gifts, pushing back the darkness. His power is superior to the power of darkness.

In 1 Corinthians 12, the apostle Paul taught concerning the gifts of the Spirit. Here are several principles about the gifts that are important for every believer to understand.

1. The gifts are manifestations of the Spirit of God.
2. Every believer has been given gifts according to the will of God.
3. The gifts are given so that believers "profit" in their Kingdom assignment.
4. The gifts are freely given to believers; they are not earned.
5. The gifts are connected to the purpose, identity and destiny God has planned for each believer.

The Gifts and Their Operation

Far too many believers are ignorant concerning the operation of the Holy Spirit's gifts. As a result, the gifts are underutilized. This lack of understanding of the gifts and their operation creates inaccuracy in flowing in the gifts of the Spirit. Those believers who understand the gifts and their operation, however, function in a higher degree of accuracy as they mature in the operation of their gifts.

The gifts of the Holy Spirit are within every believer, but for many they are lying dormant. The gifts were not given as adornments, but as weapons for us to use to advance God's mandate. As Lester Sumrall wrote in his book *The Gifts and Ministries of the Holy Spirit*, "The gifts of the Spirit are not tender little gifts. They are dynamic, dangerous and warlike."[1] Many believers don't recognize that these gifts are weapons of warfare. This leads to us underutilizing the weapons we have been given. Here are several reasons that the gifts are underutilized in many believers' lives.

1. *Lack of understanding of the operation of the gifts.* Every Kingdom ministry should provide regular teaching about the gifts and how they operate. This is one component that sets our identity apart from religious structures.

2. *Lack of opportunity to operate in the gifts.* Too many churches have a religious or exclusive hierarchal structure that impedes operation in the gifts of the Spirit. Either the environment has a religious structure that does not allow for the spontaneous flow of the Spirit, or an exclusive spirit is present that only allows certain members to flow in the gifts. In this second environment, usually only favorites of the leadership are allowed the opportunity.

3. *Lack of a conducive environment to learn about and operate in the gifts.* Believers need to be trained and activated in the operation of the gifts. Churches and ministries must create a safe environment where believers can exercise the gifts they have been given.

4. *Lack of understanding of God's will concerning the gifts.* Many believers are not established in the fact that God has freely given them the gifts of the Spirit and that it is His will that the gifts manifest through them.

Dear one, consider this: Soldiers in a natural theater of war would not consider going into battle with only some of their weaponry. No, a soldier in a natural battle carries all of his or her weapons. So must we in this spiritual war. It is imperative that you study and understand deeply the operations of the gifts of the Spirit, that you might be highly effective in the spiritual battles that confront you daily. Your battle against darkness won't end until the day you leave earth for heaven. The fact that you are reading this book demonstrates your desire to understand how to become more effective in your warfare as a believer.

God has given all believers one or more of the nine gifts of the Spirit. These gifts can be described as grace gifts since they are different from the gifts Ephesians 4:11–13 describes:

> He gave some to be apostles, prophets, evangelists, pastors, and teachers, for the equipping of the saints, for the work of service, and for the building up of the body of Christ, until we all come into the unity of the faith and of the knowledge of the Son of God, into a complete man, to the measure of the stature of the fullness of Christ.

We find here the leadership gifts that Jesus gave to the Church. He took His mantles of apostle, prophet, evangelist, pastor and teacher and gave these to the Church. I have heard some individuals explain that they possess all five of these leadership gifts, but I believe this is in error. It is true that all believers should display the apostolic, prophetic, evangelistic, pastoral and teaching nature. Yet it is inaccurate to describe this as meaning that each believer fully possesses all five headship offices. Jesus was the only one who fully operated in all five leadership gifts. He distributed these leadership gifts to the Church for the equipping, mobilizing, maturing and stabilizing of the believers. Prior to listing these gifts, the apostle Paul writes in Ephesians 4:8, "When He ascended on high, He led captivity captive, and gave gifts to men." The word *gifts* in this verse is translated in *Strong's Concordance* key #1390 as *doma*, meaning a "gift."

The word *gifts* used in 1 Corinthians 12:4–6 is translated differently from this, however: "There are various gifts, but the same Spirit. There are differences of administrations, but the same Lord. There are various operations, but it is the same God who operates all of them in all people." In the original context, the word used here for *gifts* is the word *charisma*. It includes the meaning "grace or gifts denoting extraordinary powers" (see *Strong's* key #5486). The extraordinary power to operate in certain gifts is given by the Holy Spirit.

Unlike the *doma* gift of leadership manifested as an apostle, prophet, evangelist, pastor and teacher, which is given to some, the gifts of the Spirit, *charisma*, are given to every believer. The Bible says "some" have been given *doma* gifts, yet every believer has been given *charisma* gifts. It is important to understand what gifts God has given you.

As believers flow in the gifts of the Spirit, their spiritual senses are exercised (see Hebrews 5:14). We have each been given differing gifts according to the measure of God's grace upon us. Romans 12:4–8 states,

> For just as we have many parts in one body, and not all parts have the same function, so we, being many, are one body in Christ, and all are parts of one another. We have diverse gifts according to the grace that is given to us: if prophecy, according to the proportion of faith; if service, in serving; he who teaches, in teaching; he who exhorts, in exhortation; he who gives, with generosity; he who rules, with diligence; he who shows mercy, with cheerfulness.

Dear one, you have been given a measure of grace. Don't let fear and apprehension prevent you from operating in the gifts God has given you. The apostle Paul encouraged his son in the faith, Timothy, regarding the gifts, urging him, "Don't minimize the powerful gift that operates in your life, for it was imparted to you by the laying on of hands of the elders and was activated through the prophecy they spoke over you" (1 Timothy 4:14 TPT). The fact that Paul was instructing Timothy, who was a young apostle, not to neglect the gift tells us that spiritual gifts can be neglected. God desires that all believers flow in the gifts of the Spirit.

Gifts of the Spirit

When you and I flow in the gifts of the Spirit, God arises (see Psalm 68:1). Whenever God arises, hearts are touched and lives are changed as He uses you and me to reveal Himself. Let's focus more intently for a few moments on the nine gifts of the Spirit that the apostle Paul outlined in his letter to the Corinthian Church and to us.

> But the manifestation of the Spirit is given to everyone for the common good. To one is given by the Spirit the word of wisdom, to another the word of knowledge by the same Spirit, to another faith by the same Spirit, to another gifts of healings by the same Spirit, to another the working of miracles, to another prophecy, to another discerning of spirits, to another various kinds of tongues, and to another the interpretation of tongues.
>
> 1 Corinthians 12:7–10

The gifts of the Spirit are God's supernatural power operating in believers. These nine supernatural gifts can be categorized into three groups, according to their emphasis:

- *Revelation Gifts:* word of wisdom, word of knowledge and discernment of spirits.
- *Power Gifts:* gift of faith, working of miracles and gifts of healing.

• *Utterance Gifts:* prophecy, diverse kinds of tongues and the interpretation of tongues

Revelation Gifts

Gift of a word of wisdom: The gift of a word of wisdom is revelatory insight, instruction or guidance. This gift brings insight into areas that were previously unknown. It can manifest in the form of helping solve problems where previously a solution was unseen or unknown. As an example, during counseling sessions this gift can help individuals find God's path in difficult situations. This gift is revelatory in nature and is not human wisdom.

Gift of a word of knowledge: The gift of a word of knowledge is different from a word of wisdom. Both are revelatory gifts, but they differ slightly in their function. The word of wisdom involves supernatural ability to solve a particular problem. The word of knowledge is a revelatory piece of knowledge from the mind of God about a particular thing, the earth or humanity and is for a particular season or time. A word of knowledge usually manifests during prophetic utterances. It also manifests during times of healing ministry, when God reveals various types of illnesses He desires to heal. A word of knowledge is for a specific person or people. It is not human knowledge. A word of wisdom, on the other hand, is simply knowledge you would not have otherwise been aware of, and it opens the door for the voice of the Lord to be released.

Discerning of spirits: This gift is revelatory in nature and exposes the spiritual source of an attitude, an atmosphere, a word, an individual action or a corporate environment. When this gift is in operation, it helps determine whether the source of something is human or demonic. It is not a gift of suspicion or judgmentalism. It is revelatory knowledge from God regarding the source of information. This is a key gift in determining the principalities operating over cities and regions. The gift of discernment can be used in your daily life, whether you are making decisions, negotiating a business contract or praying for your children. For example, it can help worship leaders determine God's direction for praise and worship at a given time. It is a revelatory gift that "reveals" necessary information. Discernment often works with the instinctual aspect of who we are as human beings. Yet it is not human in nature, but supernatural. The Holy Spirit bypasses human reasoning and heightens our capacity to "see" in a different way.

Power Gifts

Gift of faith: The gift of faith is the supernatural ability to believe God for impossible things. Miracles and healings manifest through the gift of faith. This gift creates a supernatural opportunity for the impossible to occur and does not have its origin in human nature. Jesus operated in this gift of faith throughout His ministry on earth. He spoke to the storm, for example, and immediately the wind ceased (see Mark 4:39). Again, every miracle Jesus performed, He performed as a man and not as God. He was our example of how to operate in the Kingdom, using the power and authority we have been given.

Working of miracles: Similar to the gift of healing, the gift of miracles operates through some believers. Aside from Jesus, just a few examples of others who have operated in this realm are Smith Wigglesworth, Kathryn Kuhlman, Oral Roberts and A. A. Allen. Even today, there are several men and women of God who have been given the gift of miracles. This gift is not limited to healing sickness or raising people from the dead. Elijah performed a miracle when he raised a widow's son (see 1 Kings 17). Elisha performed a similar miracle when he raised another widow's son from the dead (see 2 Kings 4:32–36). God used Stephen to perform great wonders and miracles (see Acts 6:8). The apostle Paul had the supernatural capacity to perform special miracles (see Acts 19:11). I have also experienced miracles happening in the lives of several women who were either barren or had multiple miscarriages. After receiving prayer, they conceived and delivered healthy babies.

Healing: The gift of healing is the supernatural power of the Holy Spirit through believers to heal the sick. A significant aspect of Jesus' ministry was healing the sick (see Matthew 14:14; Mark 1:34; Luke 4:40; 5:15). I teach that all believers have a God-given supernatural capacity to heal the sick. I base this teaching on Mark 16:18, which commands believers to heal the sick. There are believers, however, who have been given a gift of healing. As they cultivate their faith and this gift, they will see more healings manifest in their ministry. Sometimes these believers might flow in a greater anointing to heal specific diseases. My spiritual father, who has now transitioned to heaven, had a gift of healing. I saw many who were healed through his ministry, but he manifested a greater anointing to heal cancers than other diseases. In my ministry, I have witnessed the operation of the gift of healing as I have prayed for individuals. I encourage you to take opportunities to pray for people who need healing.

Utterance Gifts

Prophecy: The gift of prophecy is a gift (*charisma*) of the Spirit and is not the same as the fivefold office of a prophet (*doma*). The prophetic office is a leadership gift. The gift of prophecy as an utterance gift, however, is given for the edification, exhortation and comfort of the believers. Prophecy reveals the secrets of the heart and brings the one receiving prophecy closer to the Lord. The gift of prophecy operates by faith and is received by grace. Of all the gifts of the Spirit, prophecy has the capacity to bless more people. Paul encouraged believers to covet prophesying (see Acts 2:17; 1 Corinthians 14:1, 39; Revelation 19:10). To covet is connected to desire. Paul encouraged believers to earnestly desire to prophesy.

Gift of tongues: The gift of tongues is a prophetic message from God that a person delivers in a language he or she does not understand. This is not a language the deliverer ever learned. It does not come from the realm of the soul, but from the heart of God. Persons with the gift of tongues have a supernatural capacity to speak in various languages under the unction of the Holy Spirit. I have heard testimonies of ministers who, under the unction of the Spirit, delivered sermons in languages they had never learned. They had no idea of the content of the message until someone in the gathering who knew the language interpreted it for them. The gift of tongues should not be confused with the unknown tongues we use in our prayer times personally, when we speak directly to God using heaven's languages.

Interpretation of tongues: The interpretation of tongues is connected to the gift of tongues wherein prophecy is delivered. When a prophecy is delivered in tongues, someone with the gift of interpretation interprets the message from God. The interpretation does not involve the mental faculties of the person interpreting, but is given under the unction of the Holy Spirit.

Anywhere and Everywhere

These nine gifts of the Spirit are meant for action. God has given you your gifts to do the work of ministry wherever you go. This is a picture of Kingdom influence.

This means that the gifts are not limited to the ministry you attend. Anywhere and everywhere you go, you must develop the capacity to rebuke the darkness by revealing God's power and presence through the gifts of the Spirit.

These gifts are not your natural talent, nor are they cute adornments. These gifts are weapons of war that you and I must use to rebuke the powers of darkness holding cities, regions and nations captive.

Don't let fear stagnate you. Let faith arise in you to use the weapon of these gifts of the Spirit.

Application

Review the list of the nine gifts of the Spirit each day. Create a journal listing the gifts of the Spirit you operate in. Each day, spend time asking the Lord to open your eyes to opportunities to minister in these gifts. Make this declaration aloud each day: *I am a well-armed soldier, and I am ready for war. I am ready for God's weapons, including the gifts of the Spirit He has given me, to operate and function in my life.*

Principles and Pitfalls

Becoming effective at operating in the gifts of the Spirit involves both principles we must learn to put into practice and pitfalls we must learn to avoid. I received a portion of my prophetic training at Christian International, led by Bishop Bill Hamon, a strong apostolic leader in the Body of Christ. I learned the principles I am sharing here during that time and during my journey as I have trained and activated believers. Let's look at a few of the main principles and pitfalls we should be aware of as we operate in our God-given gifts.

The Principle of Faith and Love

Faith and love must motivate your desire to operate in the gifts of the Spirit. God has given you the gifts of the Spirit to advance His Kingdom and defeat the darkness that surrounds you. Keeping your motives pure as you operate in the gifts is key to seeing results. Purpose to walk in love. As you walk in love, your faith increases. Faith works by love (see Galatians 5:6). Faith is the "secret sauce" that helps you give yourself to the operation of the Spirit of God through you. "Faith is the substance of things hoped for, the evidence of things not seen" (Hebrews 11:1).

The Lone Ranger Pitfall

Proper alignment and connectedness to mature believers will protect you from this error that comes from isolation. You and I do not operate alone. We must walk in unity with each other and avoid this lone ranger pitfall. You and I are members of the "many membered" Body of Christ (see 1 Corinthians 12:12–31). Being one of the members of the Body is a picture of unity and alignment. We must therefore resist isolating ourselves from other believers.

The gifts you have been given are not for you. God has given you the gifts to advance His agenda, to represent Him to the people you encounter and to influence those people for the Kingdom. God created you and gave you spiritual gifts to accomplish this. Before you were born, He infused your DNA with His purposes. There is a reason He created you. Paul described believers as being part of the Body of Christ, with each member having a function. Just as every part of your natural body serves a necessary function, so it is in the Body of Christ. You and I each have a function or purpose, and we are each important to God's plan. In the same manner that the different parts of our bodies are interdependent on the other members—i.e., the foot needs the toes, the eyes need the eyelids, etc.—we members of the Body of Christ need each other, too.

The Pride Pitfall

Pride will hinder you from flowing in the full measure of the spiritual gifts God has given you. As you flow in the gifts, you must resist the spirit of pride. The gifts are God's, not ours. We have been given these gifts to advance God's agenda, not our own.

The gifts are a manifestation of God's supernatural grace operating within you and me. As James 4:6–7 (TPT) says, "But he continues to pour out more and more grace upon us. For it says, 'God resists you when you are proud but continually pours out grace when you are humble.' So then, surrender to God. Stand up to the devil and resist him and he will flee in agony." Don't allow pride to capture you. Rather, endeavor to remain humble before God.

The Principle of Who, What and Why

We can see the apostle Paul addressing the principle of identity, destiny and purpose—the who, what and why of our existence—in his letter to the Church in Ephesus:

> We have become his poetry, a re-created people that will fulfill the destiny he has given each of us, for we are joined to Jesus, the Anointed One. Even before we were born, God planned in advance our destiny and the good works we would do to fulfill it!
>
> Ephesians 2:10 TPT

Purpose, identity and destiny are linked. Together, they answer three vital questions about you. Purpose answers the question, *Why was I created?* Identity answers the question, *Who was I created to be?* Destiny answers the question, *What was I created to do?* Let's look for a moment at each of these.

The gifts of the Spirit are expressed through your identity. Discovering your identity, who God created you to be, is key to fully unlocking the gifts He has given you. Once you discover your identity, then everything you need to fulfill your destiny and purpose is attracted to you. God provides everything you need to accomplish what He has for you to do. His gifts help you walk in your destiny and purpose.

I have heard many people express frustration over a lack of understanding concerning their destiny, or what God created them to do. The first steps toward understanding your destiny actually involve understanding your identity and purpose—again, these three concepts are closely linked. If you know your identity and purpose, the *who* and the *why*, then you can discover your destiny, the *what*.

To know who you are is crucial; knowing who you are begins to shape your self-perception differently. When you identify who you are in Christ, that is the point when you gain a fuller understanding of God's plans for you. Your identity must be understood in conjunction with who Jesus is.

Along with that, God purposed you for a purpose and sent you to earth to fulfill His purpose. He had something in mind when He created you. That something, that purpose, answers the *why* of your existence.

Once you discover why God created you and who He created you to be, you can then discover your destiny—what He created you to do. God initiated your purpose, identity and destiny. Understanding these three areas and the questions they answer about you can help you build faith, knowing that God has given you what you need.

Preset and Powerful

Your identity was preset before you were born and is one of your most powerful possessions. We don't decide our destiny; we discover our destiny. In order to alter your destiny, the enemy seeks to distort your identity. He will also attempt to steal your identity through trauma. But when you know the answers to the *who*, *what* and *why* questions we just looked at, he cannot steal or distort who God created you to be.

God's purpose for your life, however, should not be your good idea of what you would like to be or do. That is how unbelievers live; they choose their own path in life. As a believer, you must access God's plan for you. This involves a process of discovery.

Perhaps you have made mistakes that you feel are insurmountable. It only appears that way. Wherever you are in life, as you submit your life to God, you are moving toward a great destiny. Where you are right now is not where your story ends. God created you intentionally; He did not create you to discard you. There is grace for your mistakes. It is time to forgive yourself and move forward.

Nothing in your life is wasted. God uses everything to move you toward the great destiny He has planned for you (see Romans 8:28). Don't lose heart, and don't quit. God's plan for you will be realized as you walk with Him, trusting Him. God is faithful, and He will heal you in the areas where you are broken. He will strengthen you in the areas where you feel weak. He has not abandoned you. Let faith come alive in you right now to receive restoration in any broken areas. It is time to be healed from disappointments, failures, rejection and anything else attempting to rule over you to keep you from fulfilling God's purpose for you.

We are at war. All Kingdom warriors have been called to war; this includes you. We have been "set" in the Body: "This is where God comes in. God has meticulously put this body together; He placed each part in the exact place to perform the exact function He wanted" (1 Corinthians 12:18 VOICE). God's destiny for your life will be consistent with the way He has wired you. God has given you clues to your unique experiences, passion, abilities and your spiritual gifts to help you to discover your identity. The spiritual gifts He has given you can operate more fully as you understand who you are and why He has given them to you.

The primary reason God has given you spiritual gifts is to bless other people by revealing His heart for them and to displace the powers of darkness that would try to hold their hearts captive. As Lester Sumrall also wrote, "The gifts of the Spirit are the weapons God gives us to fight and win our battles. We must never underestimate their strength, their power, and their usefulness; but we must study them deeply and continuously until they function through us."[2] Passive believers won't influence their sphere of authority. You must be as bold as a lion (see Proverbs 28:1). Fearless!

When you step out as part of the Ekklesia, you are never alone. God's gifts, which are manifestations of His power, are with you. Keep in mind the fact that flowing in the gifts of the Spirit reveals God, and that lives are changed as a result. Don't underestimate who you are in Christ. You are filled with the power of God, and it is time for you to rise to the next level God has planned and purposed for you.

Reflection

Reflect back on our discussion about purpose, identity and destiny. Using your journal, write a brief description of your purpose. Why has God created you? Fill in the sentence *God created me because* . . . Next, write a brief description of your identity. Who has God called you to be? A healer? A prophet? A part of the Body of Christ involved in helps and administration? Fill in the sentence *God has created me to be* . . . Now, with your answers to purpose and identity in mind, write a brief description of your destiny. Fill in the sentence *God created me to . . . for Him.* If necessary, reread the descriptions of the nine gifts of the Holy Spirit and allow the Lord to show you how He has planned for you to use these gifts as you walk in your identity to carry out your God-given purpose and fulfill your destiny.

Prayer Activation

I confess that I am filled with purpose. God was intentional when He created me. I confess that my identity is in Christ, and that as I understand who Jesus is, I will understand who I am. I decree that I will live the destiny God has planned for me. I will not deviate from His plan, in Jesus' name.

10

The Power of Influence

Go into all the world and preach the gospel to every creature. He who believes and is baptized will be saved. But he who does not believe will be condemned. These signs will accompany those who believe: In My name they will cast out demons; they will speak with new tongues; they will take up serpents; if they drink any deadly thing, it will not hurt them; they will lay hands on the sick, and they will recover.

Mark 16:15–18

In the introduction to this book, we defined *influence* as "the capacity or power of persons or things to be a compelling force on or produce effects on the actions, behavior, opinions, etc., of others."[1] When you influence someone or something, there is a measure of change that occurs. Influence initiates change. Whatever or whomever you have influenced changes in form and expression, in some manner or degree. This is what you are called to do. Another way to understand your assignment as an influencer is to recognize that you are anointed as an agent of change.

God is raising up influencers who understand their Kingdom assignment to use their power and authority to advance His mandate. You and I are called to influence those around us for the Kingdom. Dear one, I believe that you have been reading this book because you sense a call of God to do more for the Kingdom. You know that you are called to do great things, but maybe the necessary understanding of how to maximize your influence continues to elude you.

"But the people who know their God will be strong and take action" (Daniel 11:32). You are called to action and not passivity. Your Kingdom assignment to cast out demons and heal the sick requires influence. This mandate includes using your supernatural language. God did not intend you to sit on the "seat of do nothing," passively waiting for your time on earth to be over. God has given you the supernatural weapons and power to take action, overcoming darkness and influencing those within your sphere of influence.

Your sphere of influence is your environment. It is the place God has assigned you to, where you will have the greatest impact as an influencer who does great exploits for His Kingdom. Your Kingdom assignment requires you to use your influence. God's ultimate purpose is for all people to receive eternal life. "He does not want any to perish, but all to come to repentance" (2 Peter 3:9). Harvesters are influencers. The gifts and weapons you have been given supernaturally enable you to overcome vain philosophies and human arguments as you demonstrate the power and superiority of God's Kingdom.

As we discussed earlier, our motivation is love and unity. Our desire must be to reveal God's heart of love for men and women. This is influence. As you use your God-given gifts and weapons, your influence increases. As your influence increases, your Kingdom productivity also increases, enabling you to compel individuals to come into the Kingdom. "Go out to the highways and hedges, and compel them to come in, so that my house may be filled" (Luke 14:23).

Are you currently influencing individuals for God's Kingdom? Are you growing in your capacity as a Kingdom influencer? Are you maximizing your influence? If you answered no to any of these questions, here are some keys to help you to maximize your influence.

1. *Change your mindset.* This means changing your thinking about what you are called to do. You must believe that God has called and anointed you for His purposes. Wrong theology will prevent you from becoming the influencer God purposed you to be and can create an ungodly passivity within you. Renewing your mind in the Word of God aligns your thinking with God's intent.

2. *Change your self-perception.* Maximizing your influence requires you to develop self-confidence. I didn't say self-reliance. You must be totally dependent on God and not on your own abilities. Changing your self-perception will change your viewpoint. This is an essential mindset shift. You cannot maximize your influence if you don't believe in yourself. You must believe that you are capable through the power of the Spirit to become who God purposed you to be. Break free of what I call the fraud factor. When you are captured by the fraud factor, you are convinced that people will see you as a fraud. This is a form of self-rejection. Get free today.

3. *Receive fresh vision.* You must develop vision for your future. Your message is not just words. Your message is how you are presenting yourself to the world. Vision clarifies your direction. Without an ongoing revelation

of God's purposes, you will become stagnant and lose your way. Vision helps you see how to move your Kingdom assignment and grounds you in God's intent. Vision mixed with faith helps you see beyond your current circumstances and perceived inadequacies.

4. *Change your attitude.* Don't blame others for deficiencies in your life and character. Take responsibility. Evaluate your attitude. You can change your attitude by changing your thoughts. This is important because your thoughts determine your destination. What has been your attitude toward spiritual things? Identify old hurts and wounds that might be preventing your from developing a healthy attitude toward spiritual things. Be honest with yourself and with God. Submit your attitude to the Lord and let the Holy Spirit create the character of Jesus within you.

Supernatural by Design

Before you were born, God had a plan and purpose for your life. Your destiny might be a mystery to you, but it is not a mystery to Him. He has a vision of you and for you. He believes in you because He knows who He created you to be. Who you are becoming is no surprise to God, because just as with Jeremiah, He has carefully planned your future (see Jeremiah 1:5).

The enemy will try to convince you that you have no future or that you cannot become an influencer. Don't forget that Satan is a deceiver and the father of lies. The truth is that God loves you and has planned a good future for you (see Jeremiah 29:11). Your heavenly Father loved you so much that He sent Jesus to be your Redeemer so that you would have access to Him. Your access to the Father created access to live the great destiny He has planned for you.

Not only has your Father planned your future; He has also given you supernatural capacity through the Holy Spirit. You are supernatural by design, and just as God planned and purposed you, He is helping you fulfill His plans.

> Blessed be the God and Father of our Lord Jesus Christ, who has blessed us with every spiritual blessing in the heavenly places in Christ, just as He chose us in Him before the foundation of the world, to be holy and blameless before Him in love; He predestined us to adoption as sons to Himself through Jesus Christ according to the good pleasure of His will, to the praise of the glory of His grace which He graciously bestowed on us in the Beloved.
>
> Ephesians 1:3–6

You have been blessed with every spiritual blessing in Christ Jesus. God has left nothing to chance.

The Maintenance Trap

Are you advancing in your Kingdom identity, or are you living in maintenance mode? Is your territory enlarging, or are you simply doing "just enough" to get by? God has given you a measure of grace to fulfill His purposes. As you fulfill those purposes, you are also living the destiny He has planned for you. I want to encourage you to avoid a trap or snare that far too many believers succumb to. It is the snare of maintenance. To fall into the maintenance trap is to be committed to living the status quo. After all, change requires work and commitment, and some believers would rather live passively, hoping to avoid warfare. The truth is that they are not avoiding warfare; they have actually been immobilized by the kingdom of darkness. All the supernatural artillery they have been given lies dormant as they endeavor to stay away from that "warfare stuff."

I encourage you to examine your life and determine whether or not you are living in maintenance mode. Are you making territorial gains? Are you demonstrating the power and authority you have been given? You must become aggressive in your commitment to daily run the race that is set before you. As the apostle Paul put it,

> I admit that I haven't yet acquired the absolute fullness that I'm pursuing, but I run with passion into his abundance so that I may reach the purpose for which Christ Jesus laid hold of me to make me his own. I don't depend on my own strength to accomplish this; however I do have one compelling focus: I forget all of the past as I fasten my heart to the future instead. I run straight for the divine invitation of reaching the heavenly goal and gaining the victory-prize through the anointing of Jesus.
>
> Philippians 3:12–14 TPT

This passage contains several keys that will help you avoid living in maintenance mode. Let's look more closely at them.

1. *Run with passion.* Passion is defined as a strong or uncontrollable emotion. Passion is not indifferent or passive. Passion is intense desire. Not only are you to be passionate; you must *run.* Passion is a picture of fire. Running implies a sense of urgency. Running is a picture of quick movement or calculated haste. You are not running aimlessly; you are running into God's abundance. You must earnestly desire to be effective as an influencer.

2. *Commit to reaching your purpose.* Maintenance mode loses sight of purpose. Living your purpose is directly connected to completing your destiny. You have been brought into the Kingdom for *now.* There is a purpose

for which Christ apprehended you. Endeavor to discover and live that purpose.

3. *Be dependent.* Humans can become dependent on many things. Your dependency, however, is to be on Christ. Don't depend on your own strength to accomplish God's purposes. Ours is a spiritual battle that can only be won in the Spirit, with the weapons God has given us. Be active in the battle, fully reliant on Christ.

4. *Focus on the future.* The apostle Paul was compelled to turn away from his past and focus on his future. You and I must be compelled to follow his example. Don't spend your life grieving over yesterday's failures, disappointments and traumas. Get healed so you can see your future. Follow Paul's example and fasten your heart on your future. In doing so, you will be encouraged to keep moving forward.

5. *Don't give up.* Deal with your setbacks and slipups in prayer. Don't quit. Those who overcome the obstacles win the prize. There is no weapon of hell that can overpower you. You must surrender to God. Never surrender to darkness. You were created to be the light that overcomes the darkness. You are anointed to be a victor in all things.

Application

Review the list of keys to avoiding maintenance mode above. Developing these characteristics is linked with your ability to continue moving forward as a next-level believer. Which of these characteristics are strongest in you? Which need more development? How do you see God developing you in these areas? Where are you resisting development? Write your responses in your prayer journal and commit to praying over areas where you are underdeveloped or where you are resisting.

Anointed and Deployed

You are a victor because Christ has conquered all things and God the Father has placed them under His feet. Christ is our example and the Head of the Church. We are the Body of Christ. That means that all things are under our feet. Temptations will come, but like Christ, you can overcome. Jesus Himself prayed for us to be kept from the power of the enemy. You can be kept from Satan's power. Here are a few Scriptures to help you overcome when you are under attack (all taken from The Passion Translation):

> I am not asking that you remove them from the world, but I ask that you guard their hearts from evil, for they no longer belong to this world any more than I do.
>
> Your Word is truth! So make them holy by the truth. I have commissioned them to represent me just as you commissioned me to represent you. And now I dedicate myself to them as a holy sacrifice so that they will live as fully dedicated to God and be made holy by your truth.
>
> And I ask not only for these disciples, but also for all those who will one day believe in me through their message.
>
> John 17:15–20

> And he alone is the leader and source of everything needed in the church. God has put everything beneath the authority of Jesus Christ and has given him the highest rank above all others. And now we, his church, are his body on the earth and that which fills him who is being filled by it!
>
> Ephesians 1:22–23

> The Lord Yahweh, Commander of Angel Armies, makes this solemn decree: "Be sure of this: Just as I have planned, so it will be. Every purpose of my heart will surely come to pass. . . . This is the plan that I have determined for the entire world.

I will accomplish it by the demonstration of my mighty power throughout the earth!" For the Lord Yahweh, the Commander of Angel Armies, has an amazing strategy, and who can thwart him? When he moves in power, who can stop him?

Isaiah 14:24, 26–27

God's purposes and plans will not fail. Jesus has conquered principalities, powers and demons. The kingdom of darkness has been defeated. No matter what we see happening in the world, Satan has been defeated. As next-level believers, you and I are anointed and deployed to enforce the victories of Christ.

Reflection

Remember our definition of *influence* at the start of this chapter—"the capacity or power of persons or things to be a compelling force on or produce effects on the actions, behavior, opinions, etc., of others." Describe your influence. Where do you see your influence having the greatest effect? In what areas does your influence need to increase?

Prayer Activation

Lord, I ask for You to bless every endeavor that I have started according to Your purpose. Let my influence increase so that I can fulfill the destiny You have planned for me. I am a Kingdom influencer, and I decree that there will be displays of power and authority in my life that will result in an abundant Kingdom harvest, in Jesus' name.

Conclusion

There are only two divisions in the invisible spiritual war that we are all engaged in. Jesus said, "He that is not with me is against me" (Luke 11:23). You cannot be neutral in this spiritual war. You are on one side or the other. Some believers, because of their fear of confrontation with the enemy, try to ignore the war and form a truce with Satan. They think if they ignore him, he will not bother them. This is one of Satan's main strategies. He is a terrorist. He tries to render members of God's army immobile by his terror tactics, filling you with fear, anxiety, doubt and other negative emotions. These negative emotions are not only toxic to your advancement; they are also paralytics designed to prevent you from advancing.

Jesus fully represented how we are to operate by faith in Kingdom principles. The world needs Christ, and its people need Him now. From generation to generation, the goal of both kingdoms has been the same—expansion. God wants humanity to respond to His love by submitting their lives to Him.

The kingdoms of this world do not currently reflect God. Mankind's attempts to correct the evils of this world through education, legislation, improving the environment and other similar methods have failed. The evils of the world continue because the problem is not natural. It is spiritual, and spiritual problems can only be resolved with spiritual measures.

As you fulfill the great destiny that God has planned for you, you become a navigator to the solution. Those around you will see Christ at work in you and through you as you walk in power and authority. As we have discussed in this book, the gifts of the Spirit, working through you, reveal God. Yes, you push back the darkness as you worship, war and win, but more importantly, you reveal God.

Satan fights to maintain control of the kingdoms of the world. He does not want them to come under God's authority. You have been raised up for this time as a Kingdom influencer who is anointed with supernatural capacity. Fulfilling your assignment requires you to utilize all the weapons and gifts God has given you.

Gaining Heaven's Perspective

We are at war against the kingdom of Satan. This war continues from generation to generation of humanity. But there is no neutrality in this war. You decide where you will fight, and against whom. Where will you take your place in this battle?

The same spiritual battle of the ages continues today, but instead of fighting the enemy, believers are often focused on building great church buildings, producing musical dramas, holding fellowship meetings and fighting one another—while this great spiritual battle wages all around them. Satan has even intensified his attacks against a Church that has withdrawn from the front lines of battle.

In this war, you will either overcome or be overcome. The alarm has been sounded. You have been called up for deployment. How will you respond? Will you stand in faith, wielding your weaponry against the powers of darkness as you follow

God's battle plan? Will you maximize your gifts and anointings to fulfill God's mandate? Will you endeavor to gain fresh revelation and war strategies that will bring forth victory? Or will you succumb to maintenance mode? Again, the alarm has been sounded. It is time for us as next-level believers to come up higher so we can gain heaven's perspective. Without the vantage point of heaven, we cannot overcome the darkness. We are seated in heavenly places with Christ. This is how we gain heaven's perspective.

Prophetic Epilogue

In 1939 Smith Wigglesworth prophesied to Lester Sumrall about the final wave of God's glory: "After the third wave," he started sobbing. "I see the last day revival that's going to usher in the precious fruit of the earth. It will be the greatest revival this world has ever seen! It's going to be a wave of the gifts of the Spirit. The ministry gifts will be flowing on this planet earth. I see hospitals being emptied out, and they will bring the sick to churches where they allow the Holy Ghost to move."[1]

On a Sunday morning during one of our corporate gatherings, the Lord showed me a picture of a high cliff. I then heard the word *precipice* from Him. I immediately opened my dictionary to confirm the meaning of the word. I discovered that a precipice is a very steep rock face or cliff. As I pondered this, I could see the battle. The Lord spoke and said,

This war season will be more intense than previous battles. It is important for My Church to gain new war strategies for this season. My Church must come up to the next level. The darkness of this season will increase significantly. Evil will increase. No longer are darkness and evil content to hide in the darkness. Now darkness is emerging as light. The darkness and evil that parents allow will capture their children. I am calling parents back to stewardship of the lives of their children from My perspective. I will give you wisdom, war strategies and joy for this time. You will overcome by the blood of the Lamb and the words of your testimony.

Even now as I write this, I hear the Lord speaking these words:

Do not forget that Satan transforms himself as an angel of light [2 Corinthians 11:4]. The darkness is deceptive, for many think the darkness is light. I am increasing discernment and revelation in this hour. Move with Me and you will overcome. Don't be ensnared by unbelief and think that I cannot help you to win. Is there anything too hard for Me? Open your eyes and see beyond the place you currently stand, and you will see Me.

The book of Revelation begins with John's visitation from heaven, in spite of his captivity on the island of Patmos (see Revelation 1:9–10). God shows John the condition of the seven churches in Asia. John receives this "prophetic download" and is commanded to write what he is shown and send it to the churches. Interestingly, in Revelation 4:1, John is invited to "Come up here, and I will show you things which must take place after this."

God has chosen you to come up to the next level. How will you respond? Will you accept His invitation to meet Him at the next level? Will you become a next-level believer?

Notes

Introduction

1. Dictionary.com, s.v. "influence," accessed July 15, 2021, https://www.dictionary.com/browse/influence.

Chapter 1 The War of Kingdoms

1. Kenneth Hagin, *Man on Three Dimensions: Volume 1 of the Spirit, Soul, and Body Series* (Broken Arrow, Okla.: Kenneth Hagin Ministries, 1973), 13.

2. Hagin, *Man on Three Dimensions*, 18.

3. Venner J. Alston, *Next-Level Spiritual Warfare: Advanced Strategies for Defeating the Enemy* (Minneapolis: Chosen Books, 2019), 41.

Chapter 2 Our Supernatural Identity

1. All *Strong's Concordance* key word definitions throughout are taken from the *Online Strong's Concordance and Lexicon* found on the EliYah Ministries website under the Resources tab. Visit https://eliyah.com/resources to find out more or to look up the individual words I discuss.

2. For more on this meaning, see *Strong's Concordance* key #649, *apostellō*.

3. Barbara Yoder, *Mantled with Authority: God's Apostolic Mandate to Women* (Colorado Springs: Wagner Publications, 2003), 96.

4. Alain Caron, *Apostolic Expansion: The Kingdom War for Territorial Gains* (Gatineau, Quebec: Réseau Apostolique Hodos, 2019), 40.

5. Adam Clarke, *Clarke's Commentary: Matthew–Revelation* (Nashville: Abingdon, 1977), 422.

6. All *Vine's Expository Dictionary of New Testament Words* definitions throughout are taken from the online version at *Blue Letter Bible*. To find out more or to look up the individual words we discuss, visit https://www.blueletterbible.org.

Chapter 3 The Ruling Church

1. Adam Clarke, *Clarke's Commentary: Matthew–Revelation* (Nashville: Abingdon, 1977), 171.

2. Ed Silvoso, *Ekklesia: Rediscovering God's Instrument for Global Transformation* (Minneapolis: Chosen, 2014), 20.

3. Leland Ryken, James C. Wilhoit, and Tremper Longman III, eds., *Dictionary of Biblical Imagery* (Downers Grove, Ill.: InterVarsity, 1998), 147.

4. For more from *Vine's Expository Dictionary of New Testament Words* on this definition of fear as reverence for God, visit https://www.blueletterbible.org/lexicon/g5401/kjv/tr/0-1/.

5. Silvoso, *Ekklesia*, 20.

Chapter 4 The Era of Apostles and Apostolic Believers

1. John Eckhardt, *Moving in the Apostolic: How to Bring the Kingdom of Heaven to Earth*, rev. and upd. ed. (Minneapolis: Chosen Books, 2017), 19.

2. David Cannastraci, *The Gift of Apostle: A Biblical Look at Apostleship and How God Is Using It to Bless His Church Today*, (Ventura, Calif.: Regal, 1996), 85.

3. John Eckhardt, *Dictionary of the Apostolic* (Chicago: Crusader's Ministries, 2002), 10.

4. Eckhardt, *Dictionary of the Apostolic*, 128.

5. Leland Ryken, James C. Wilhoit, and Tremper Longman III, eds., *Dictionary of Biblical Imagery* (Downers Grove, Ill.: InterVarsity, 1998), 700.

6. "Reform Movements 1800s," *National Geographic* Resource Library Collection, https://www.nationalgeographic.org/topics/resource-library-reform-movements-1800s/?q=&page=1&per_page=25.

7. C. Peter Wagner, *The New Apostolic Churches* (Ventura, Calif.: Regal, 1998), 49.

Chapter 5 The Era of the Prophetic Company

1. John Eckhardt, *Dictionary of the Apostolic* (Chicago: Crusader's Ministries, 2002), 21.

2. Paula Price, *Biblical Prophetics, Book 1* (Hillside, N.J.: Everlasting Life Ministries, 1994), 22.

3. Some of these thoughts are drawn from Price, *Biblical Prophetics, Book 1*, 22.

4. Price, *Biblical Prophetics, Book 1*, 24.

Chapter 6 The Force of the Anointing

1. Leland Ryken, James C. Wilhoit, and Tremper Longman III, eds., *Dictionary of Biblical Imagery* (Downers Grove, Ill.: InterVarsity, 1998), 33.

2. This prayer activation is taken from page 49 of my book *Breakthrough Prayers, Decrees and Confessions: Overcoming Demonic Resistance through Warfare Prayer* (VJ Alston International Ministries, 2019).

Chapter 7 Supernatural Weapons

1. *Encyclopaedia Britannica Online*, s.v. "Rules of engagement," accessed July 15, 2021, https://britannica.com/topic/rules-of-engagement-military -directives.
2. Adam Clarke, *Clarke's Commentary: Matthew–Revelation* (Nashville: Abingdon, 1977), 553.

Chapter 8 The Weapon of Faith

1. Bible Gateway keyword search, s.v. "fruit," accessed July 15, 2021, https:// www.biblegateway.com/quicksearch/?search=fruit&version=MEV&search type=all.

Chapter 9 Supernatural Capacity

1. Lester Sumrall, *The Gifts and Ministries of the Holy Spirit* (New Kensington, Penn.: Whitaker House, 1982), Kindle edition, chapter 3, paragraph 6.
2. Sumrall, *Gifts and Ministries*, chapter 3, paragraph 8.

Chapter 10 The Power of Influence

1. Dictionary.com, s.v. "influence," accessed July 15, 2021, https://www .dictionary.com/browse/influence.

Conclusion

1. This Smith Wigglesworth quote appears many places online; my source was Facebook: https://m.facebook.com/BobVineyard.org/photos/a.1711389 90098334/907237469821812/?type=3&_rdr.

Dr. Venner J. Alston travels internationally to communicate hope and offer Kingdom solutions for individual and societal issues. She is a commissioned apostle, gifted author, teacher and speaker.

In addition to earning a doctoral degree in Urban Education from the University of Wisconsin–Milwaukee, Dr. Alston is certified as a life coach with several organizations, including the John Maxwell Group. She is a member of the International Coaching Federation (ICF) and also holds a certification in Women in Leadership from Cornell University.

Dr. Alston is founder and apostle of Global Outreach Ministries and Training Center and The Exceptional Woman mentoring and ministry group. She hosts *Destiny Moments with Dr. Venner Alston* on Sid Roth's It's Supernatural Network. She is also aligned with Global Spheres Inc., led by apostle Chuck Pierce.

Dr. Alston lives in Milwaukee, Wisconsin, and is the author of other books, including *Breakthrough Prayers, Decrees and Confessions: Overcoming Demonic Resistance through Warfare Prayer* (VJ Alston International Ministries, 2019), and *Image Bearer: Restoring the Power and Truth of the Image of God within You* (VJ Alston International Ministries, 2020).

To discover additional resources or to sign up for Dr. Alston's free newsletter, visit www.drvjalston.org.

To book Dr. Alston to speak at your upcoming event, send your inquiry to booking@drvjalston.org.

More from Venner J. Alston

When God doesn't seem to be listening or acting, even after we pray continually, what do we do? Focusing on two areas of spiritual warfare—restoration and retribution—you will learn how to pray more effectively and receive justice for what was taken or destroyed by the kingdom of darkness. Take up your arms and fight!

Next-Level Spiritual Warfare

 Stay up to date on your favorite books and authors with our free e-newsletters. Sign up today at chosenbooks.com.

 facebook.com/chosenbooks

 @Chosen_Books

 @chosen_books